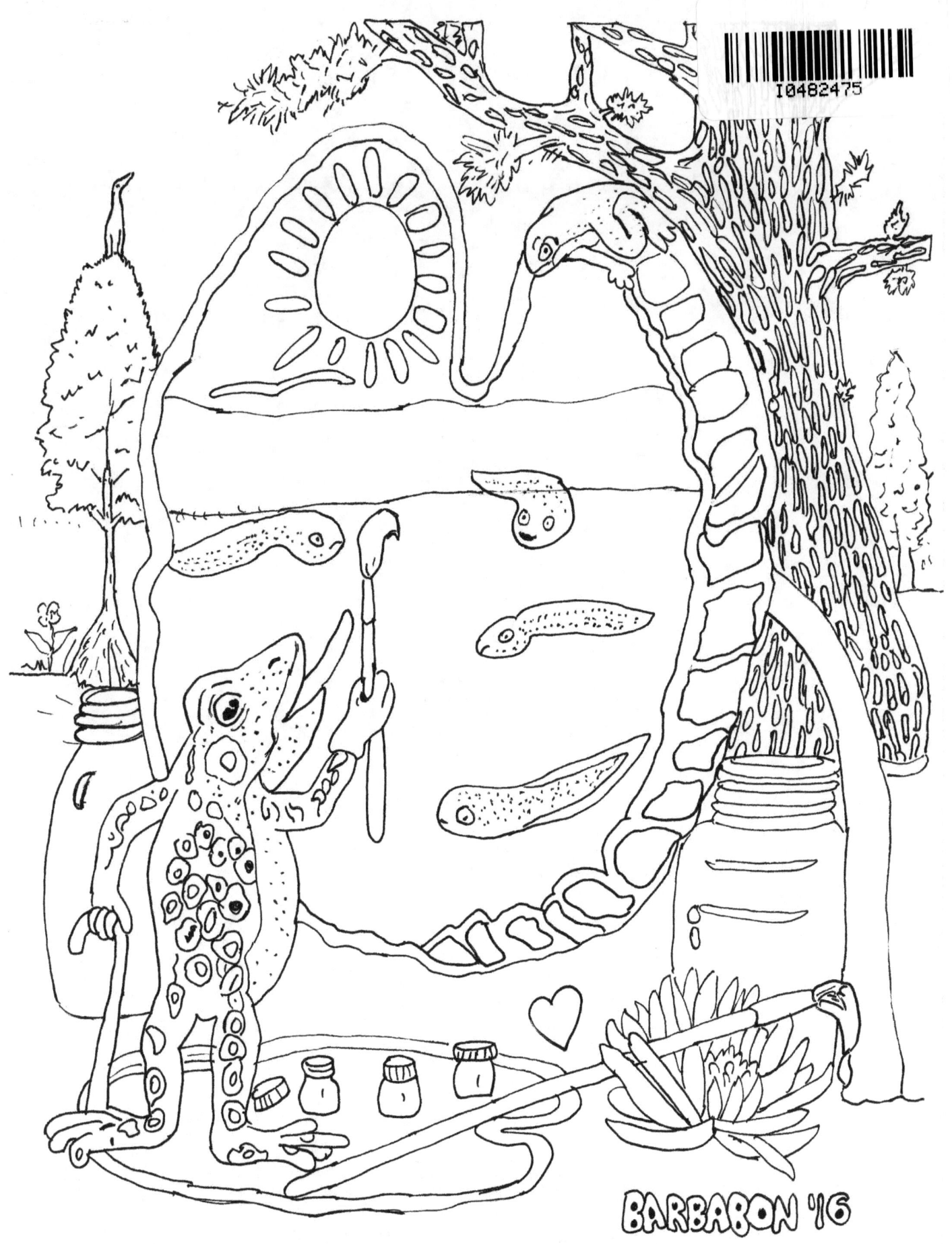

BARBABON '16

Grandma Bullfrog Paints Her Grandkids

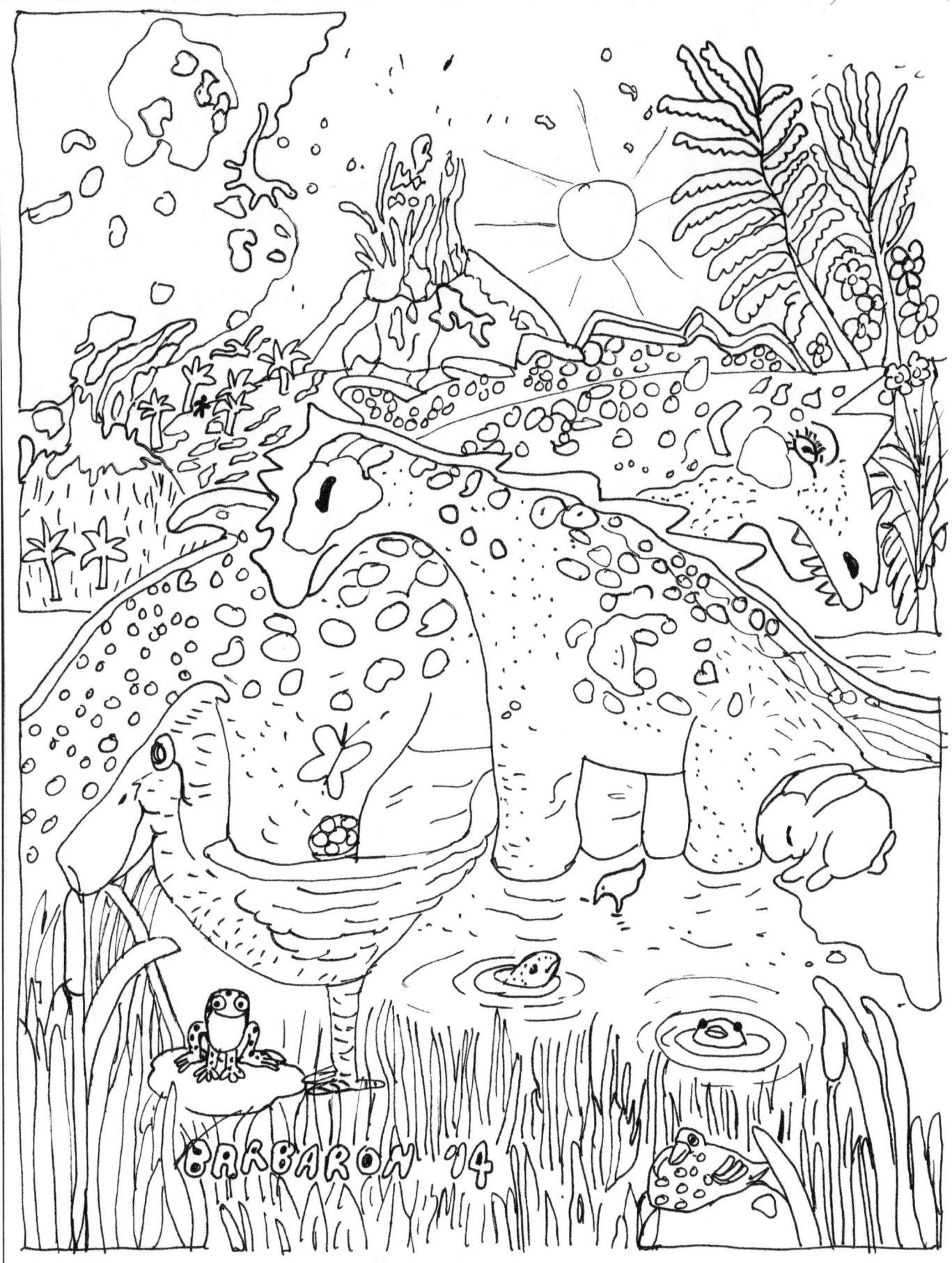

Butterfly Tattoo

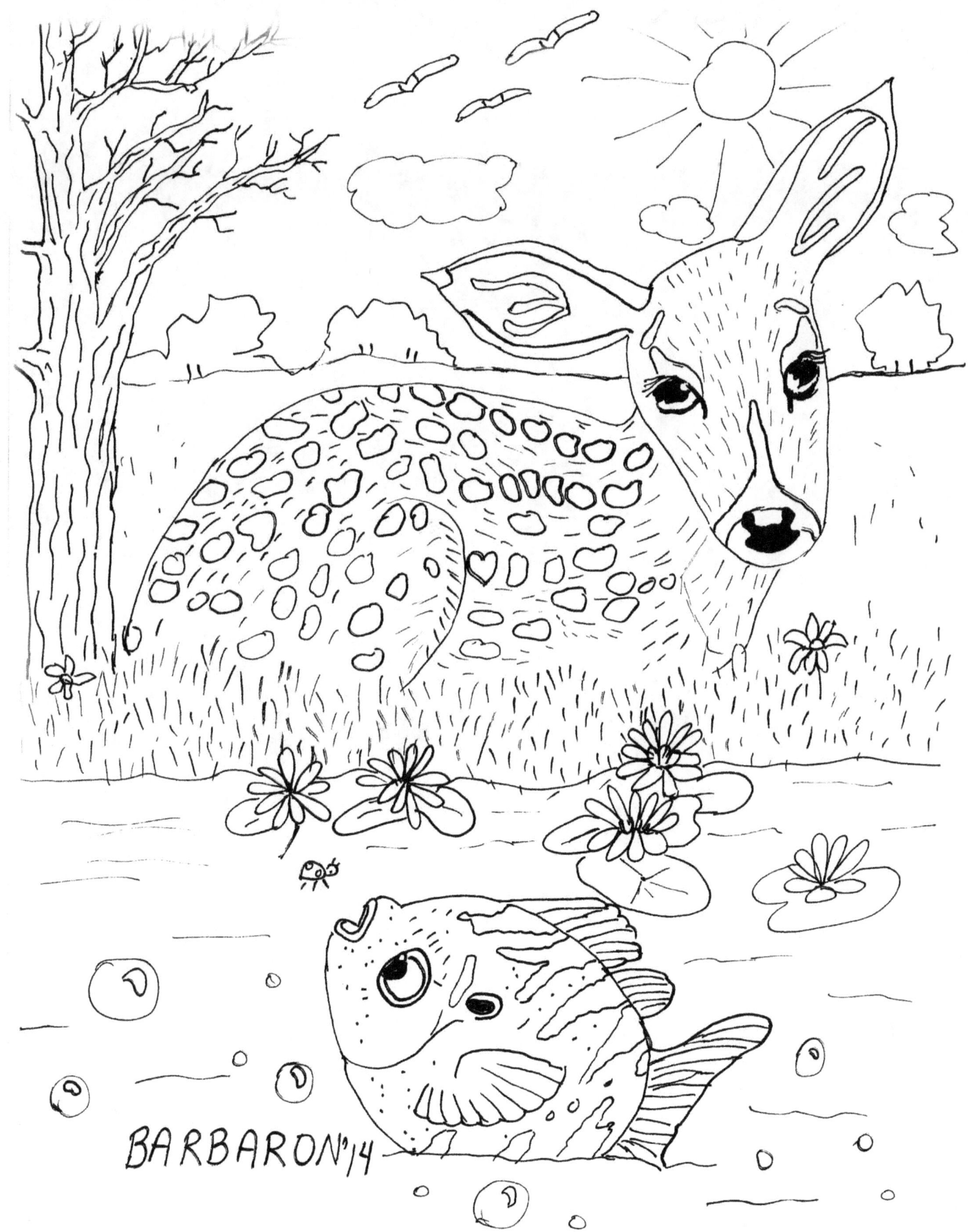
BARBARON '14

The Innocents

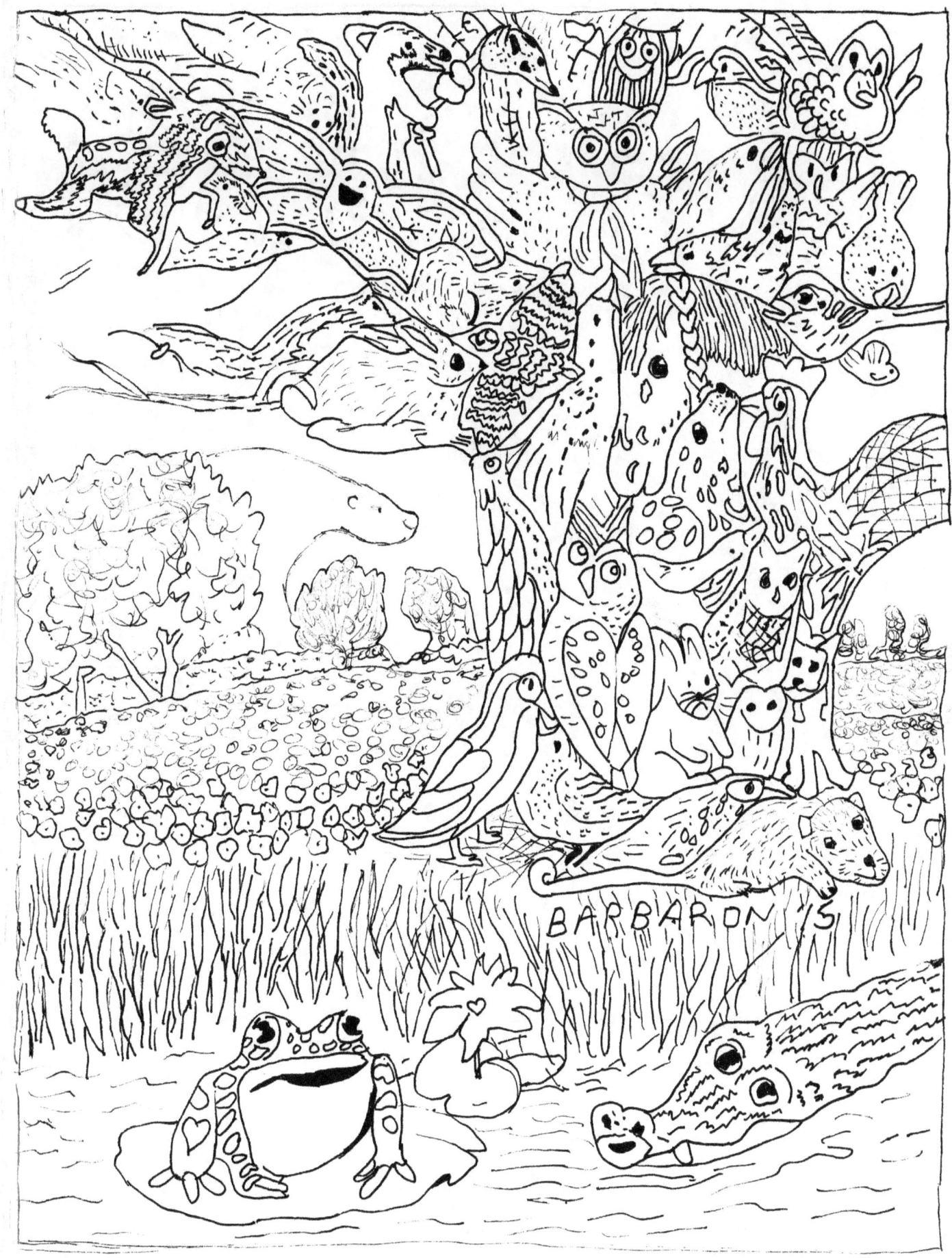

Frog Story

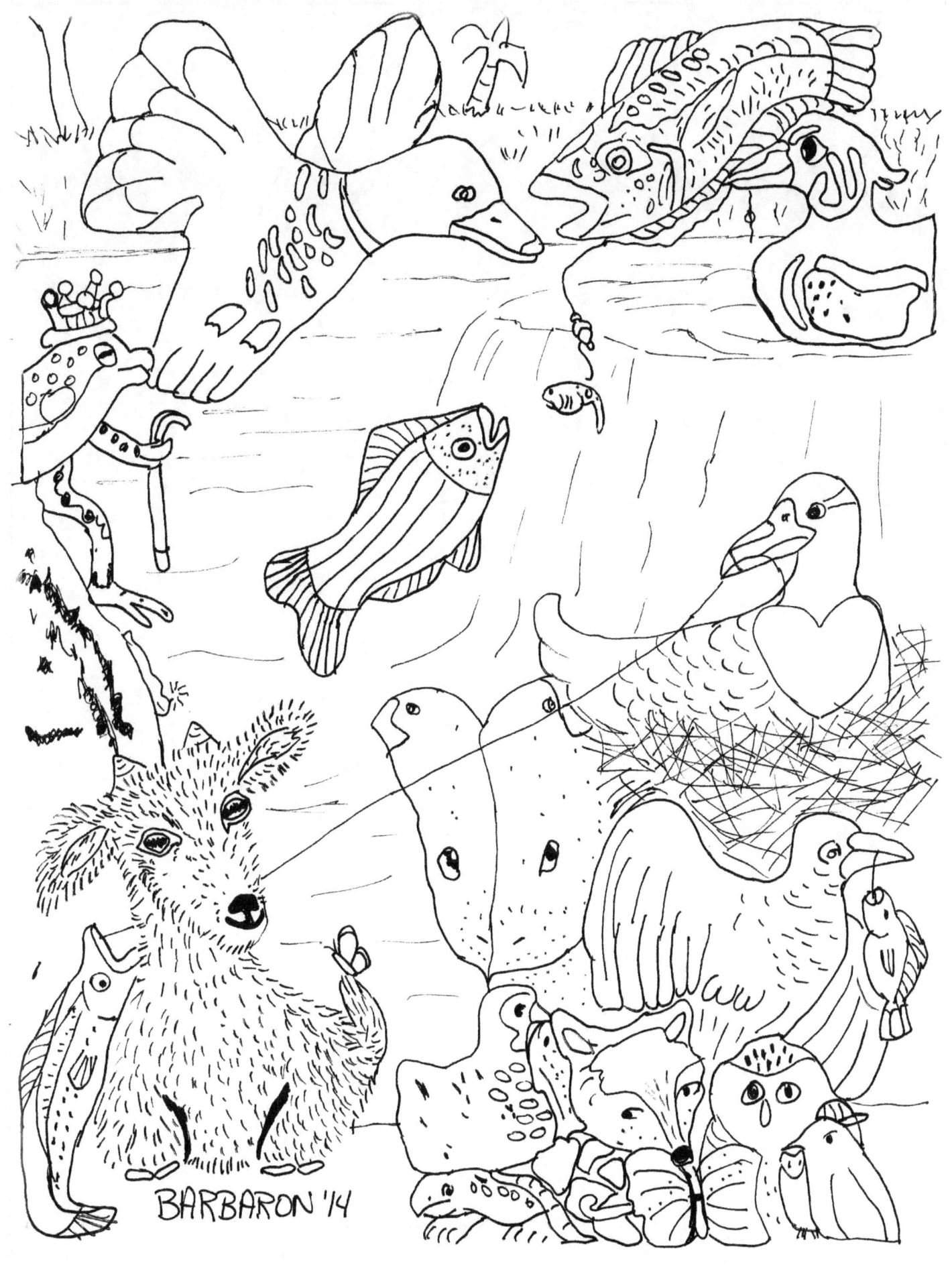

King Frog & His Fishing Ducks

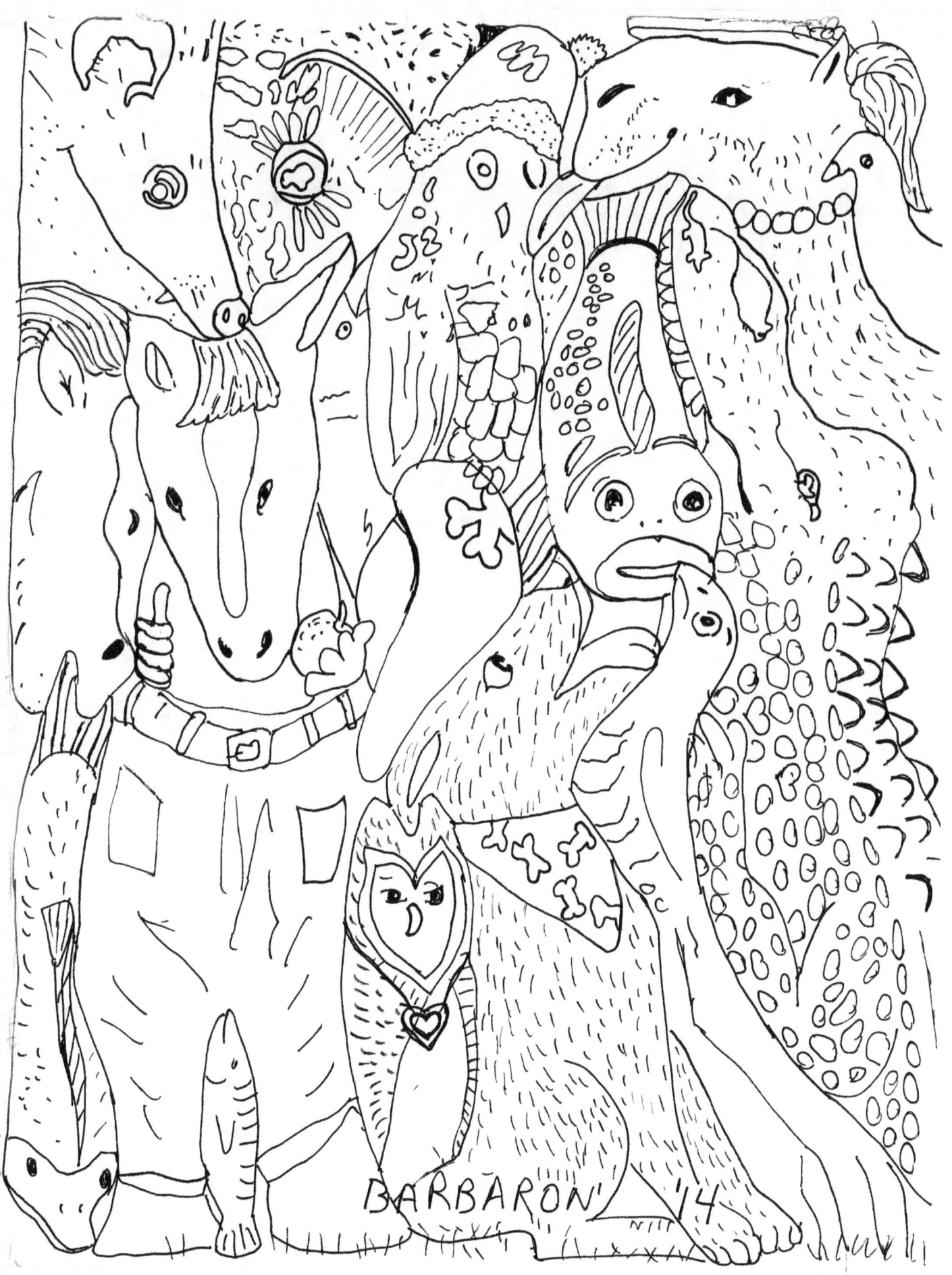

Pirate Dog & His Misfit Crew

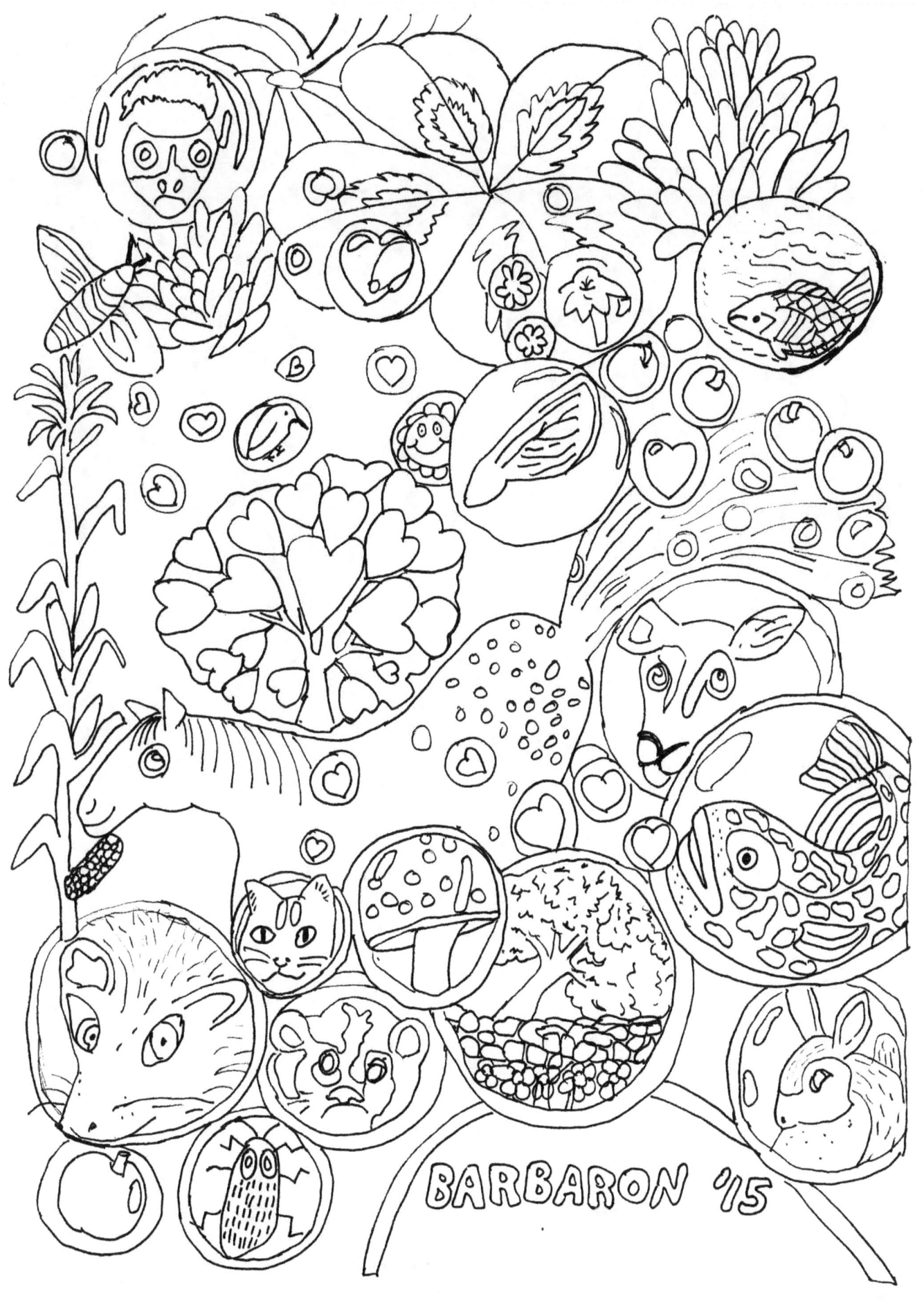

Lucky Bubbles

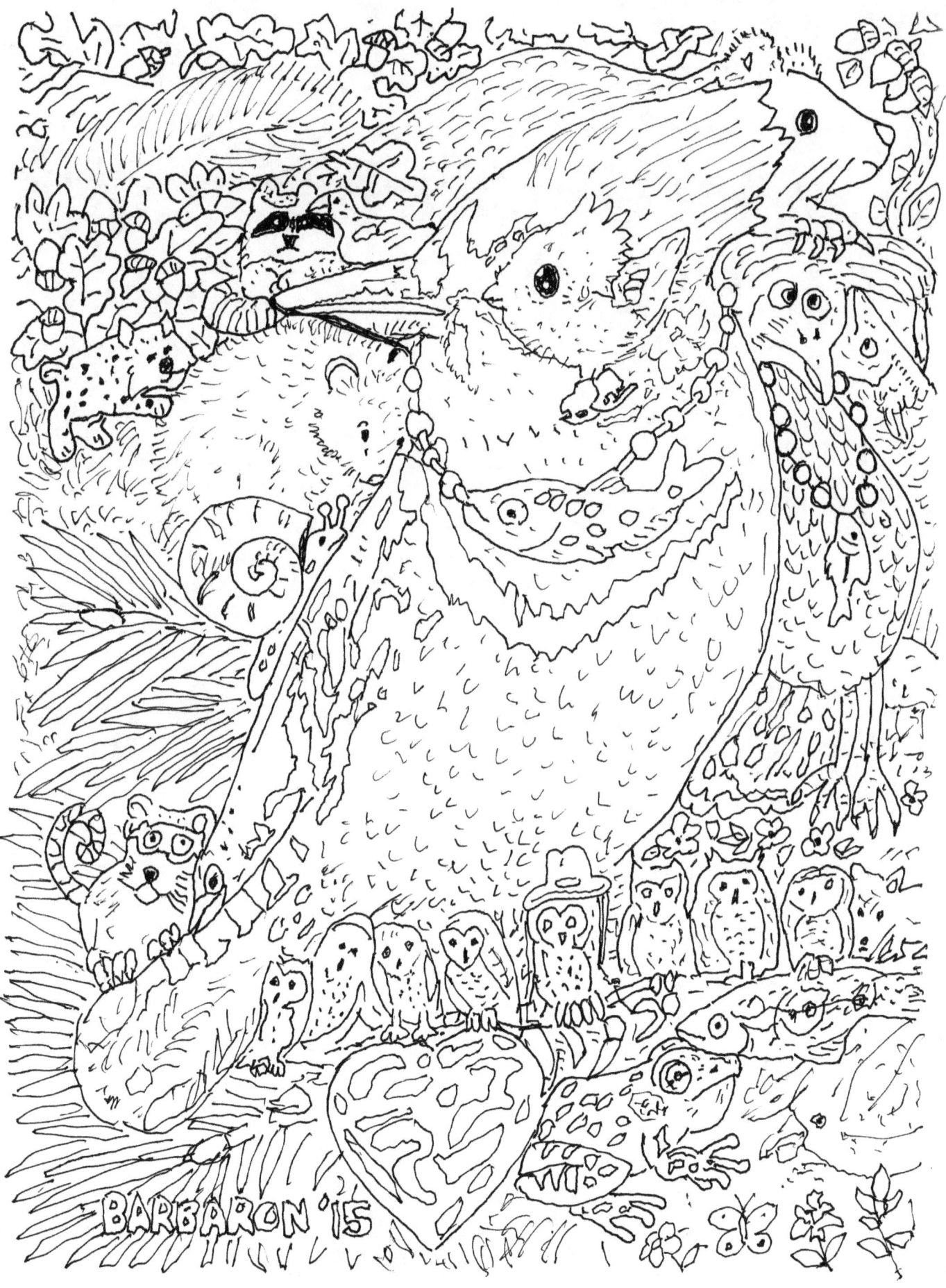

BARBARON '15

The Blue Jay with a Fish Necklace

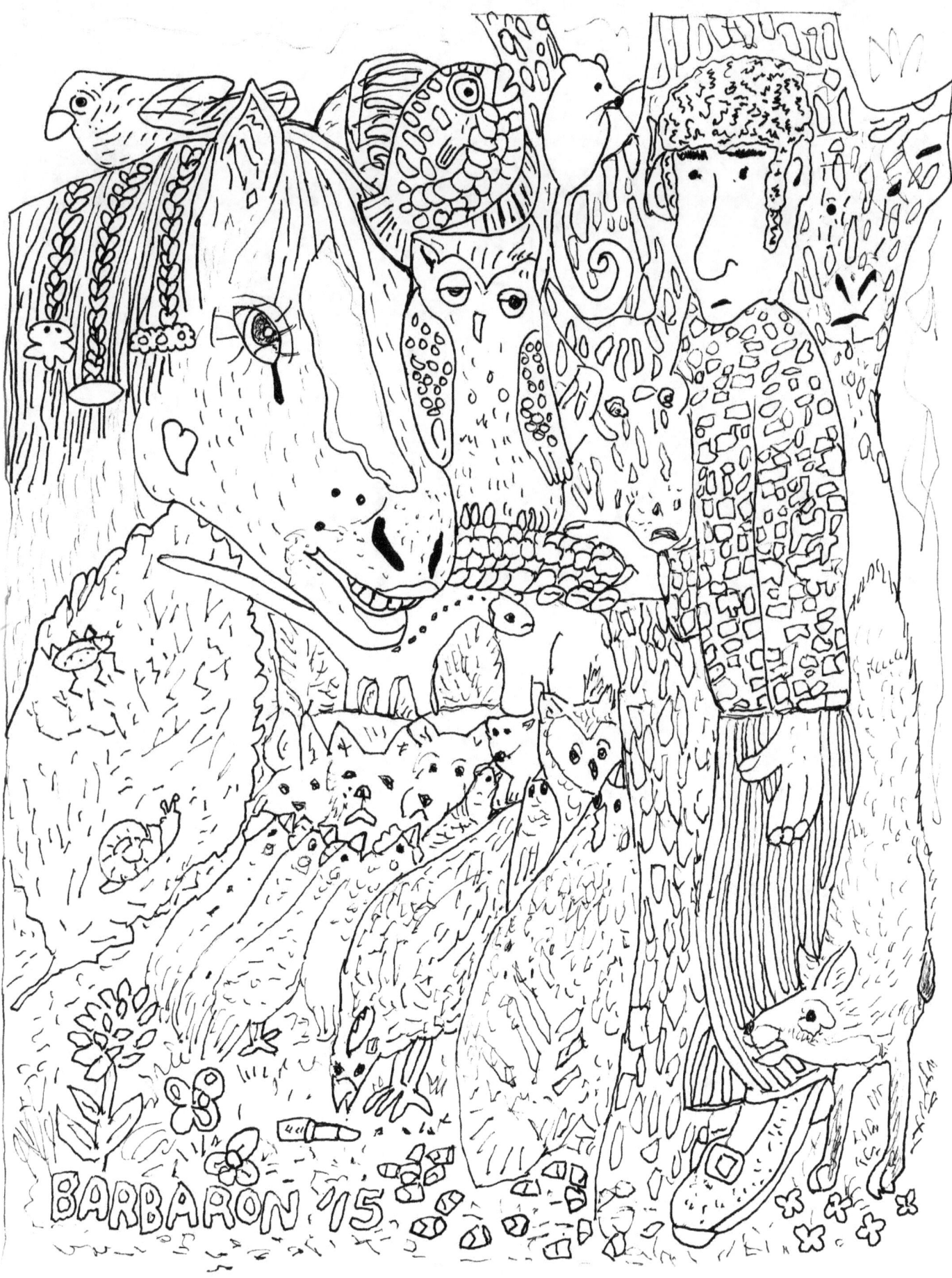

Dr. Featherday's Farm

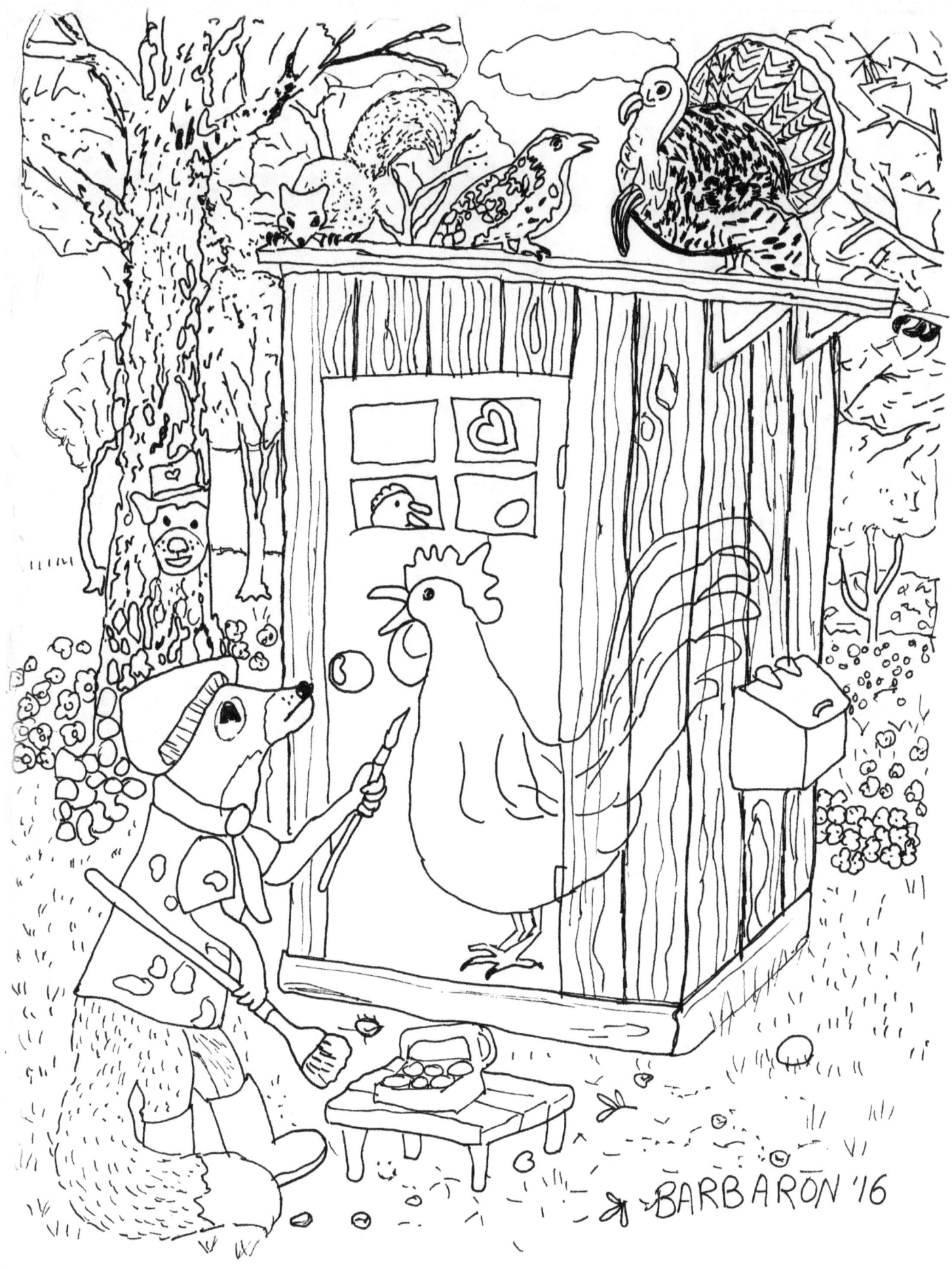

Fox Paints His Favorite Bird

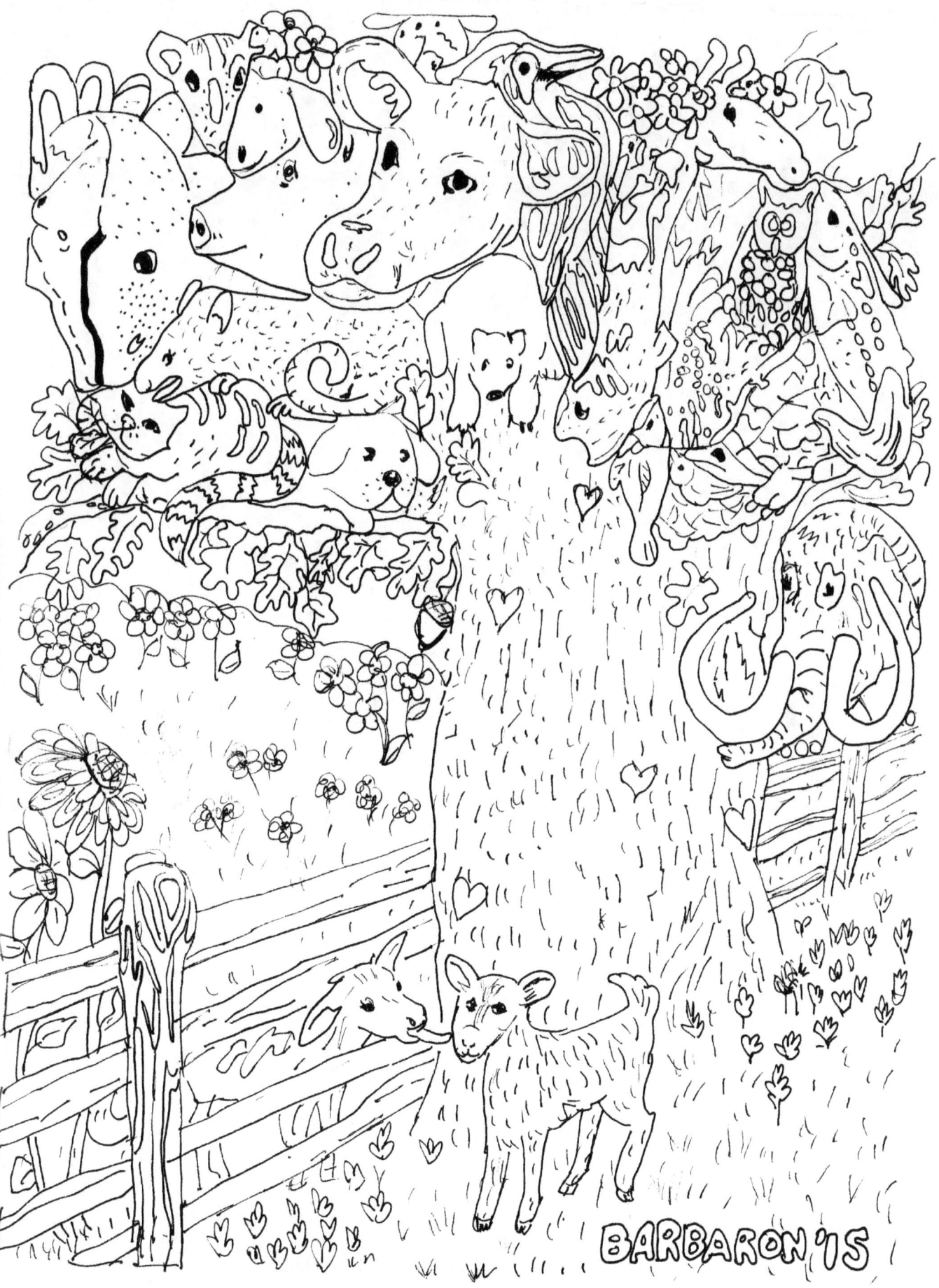

Meeting Under the Whispering Oak

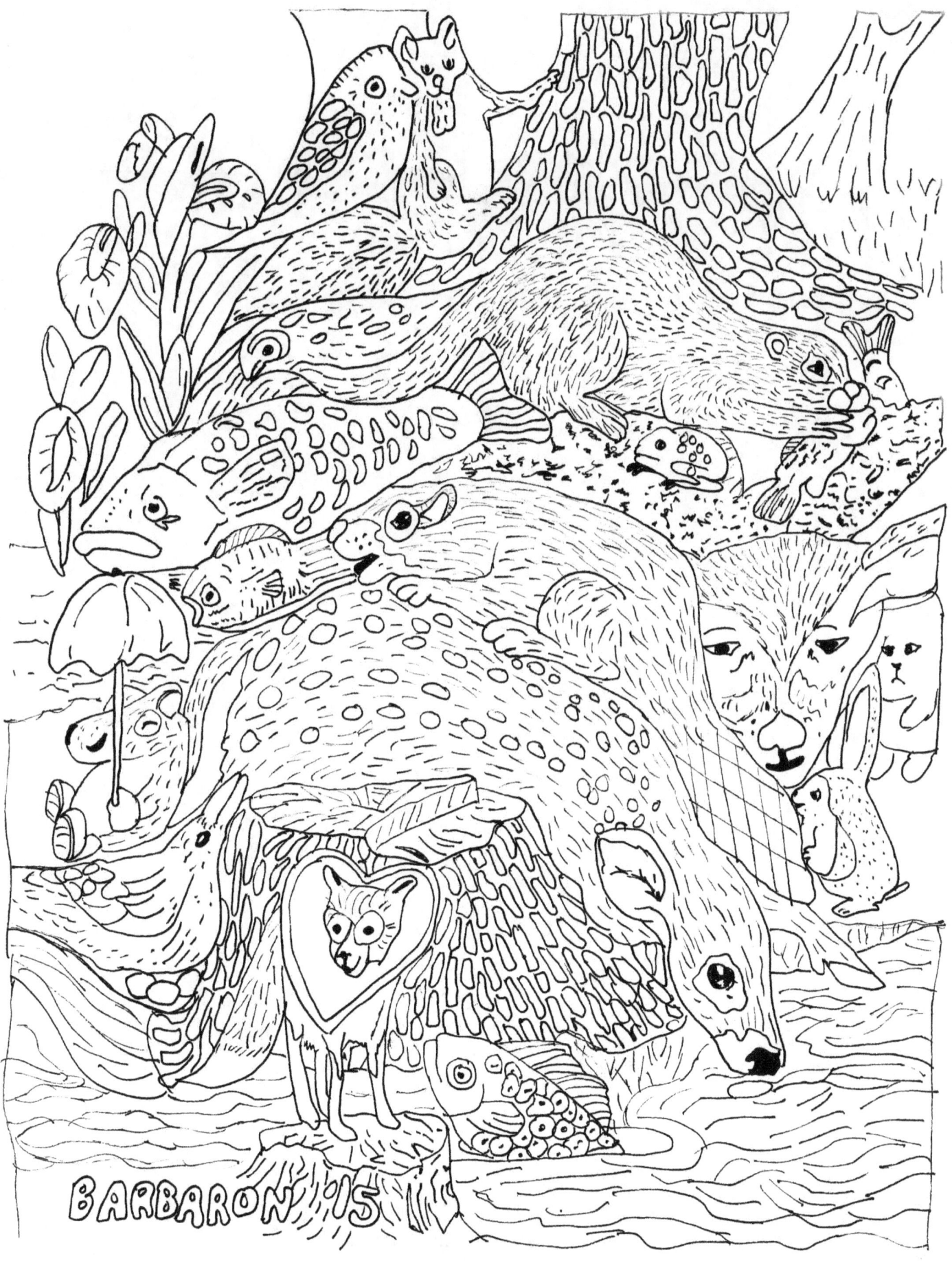

BARBARON '15

Day Dreams of the Umbrella Bear

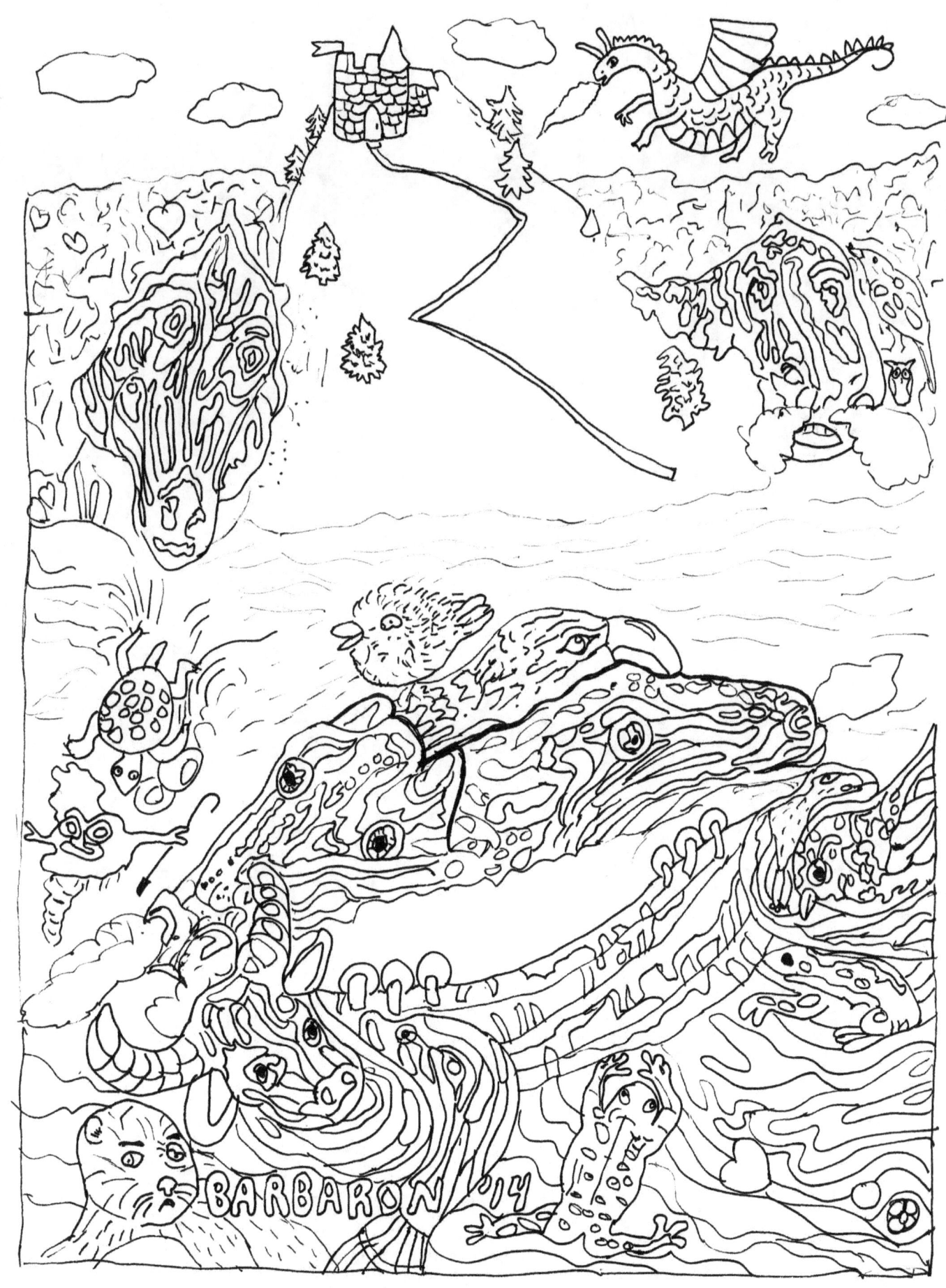

The Princess' Pet Dragons

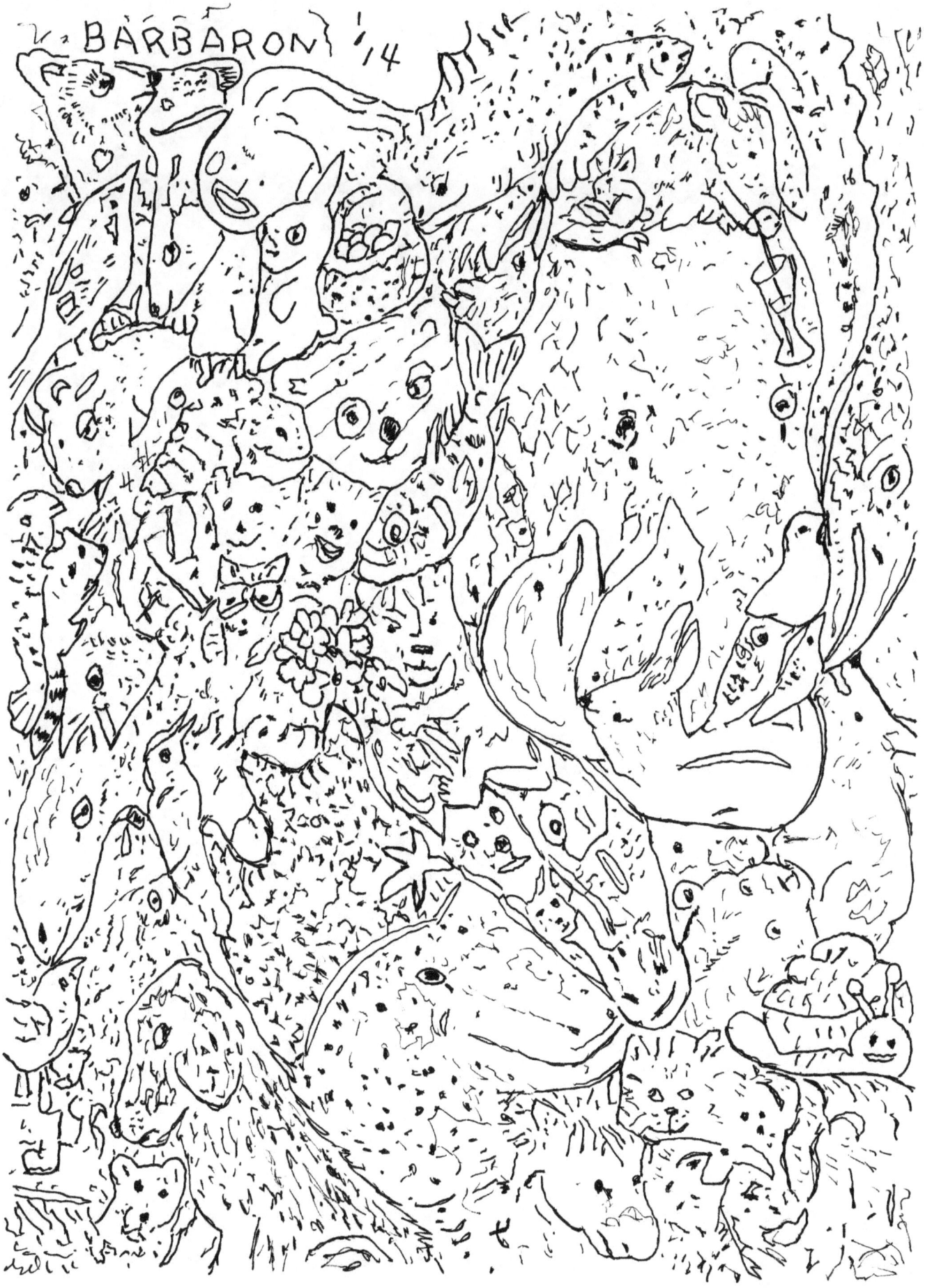

King Lizard & His Wacky Posse

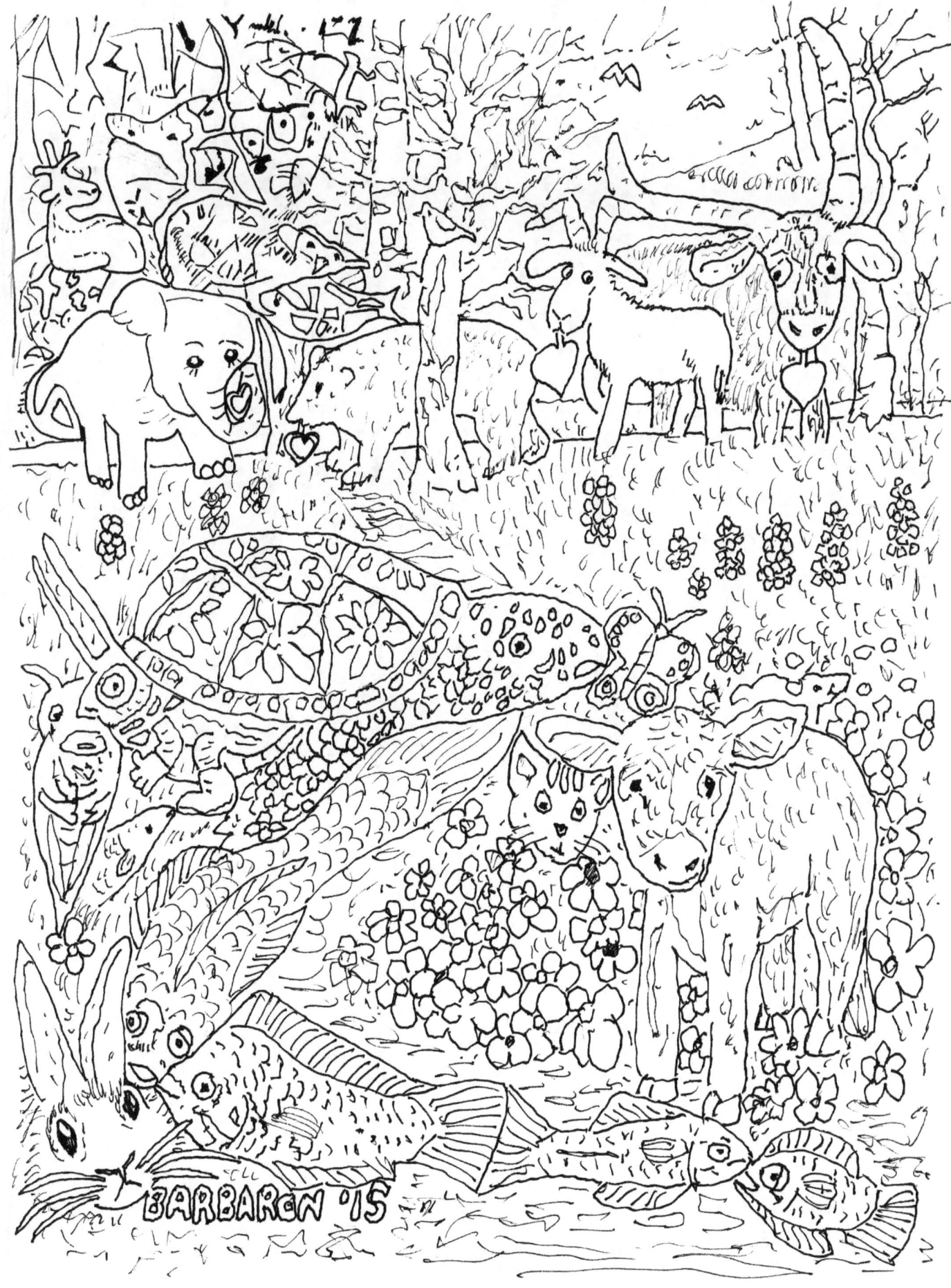

The Fish Trail

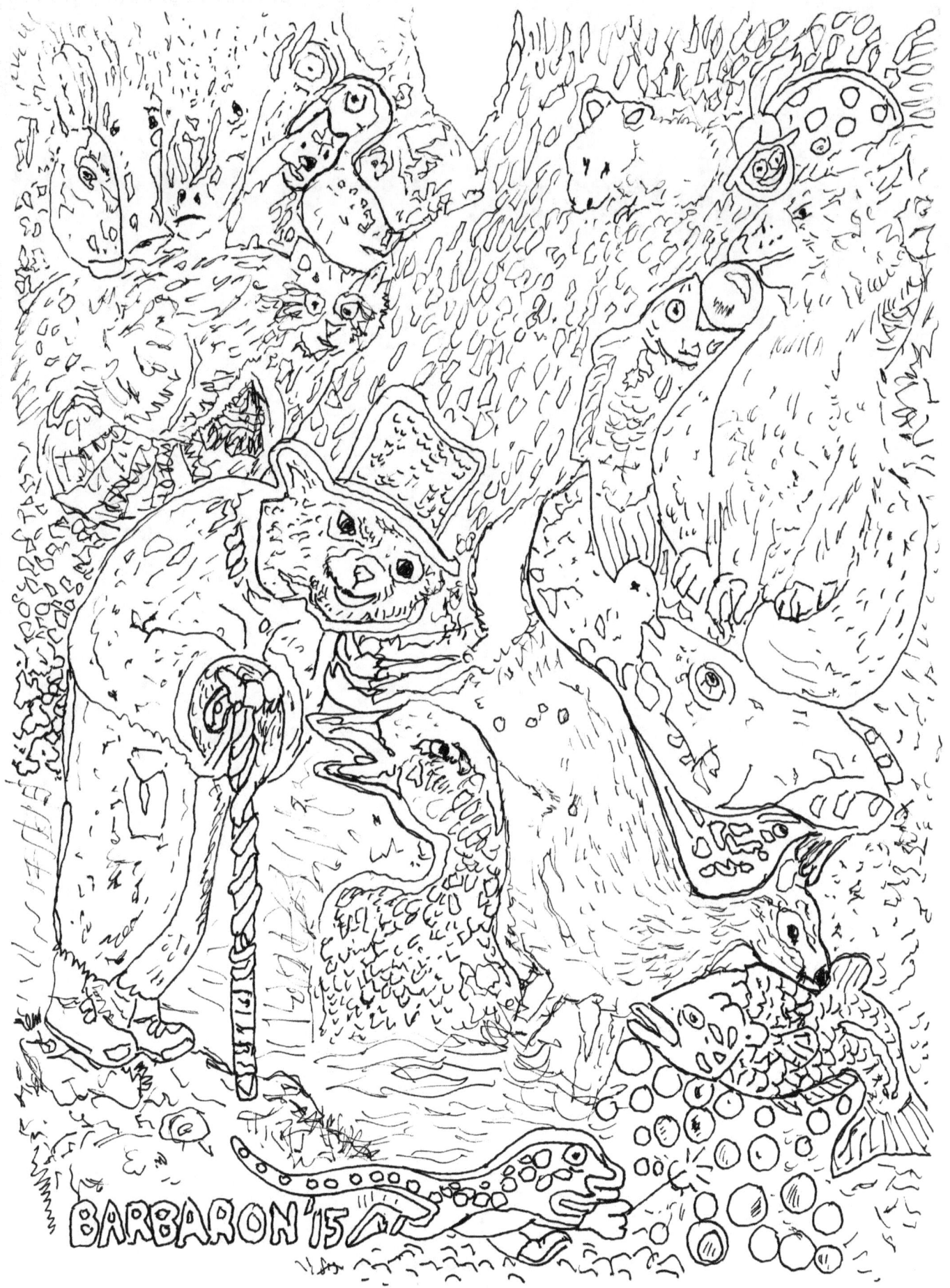

Woodchuck with a Cane

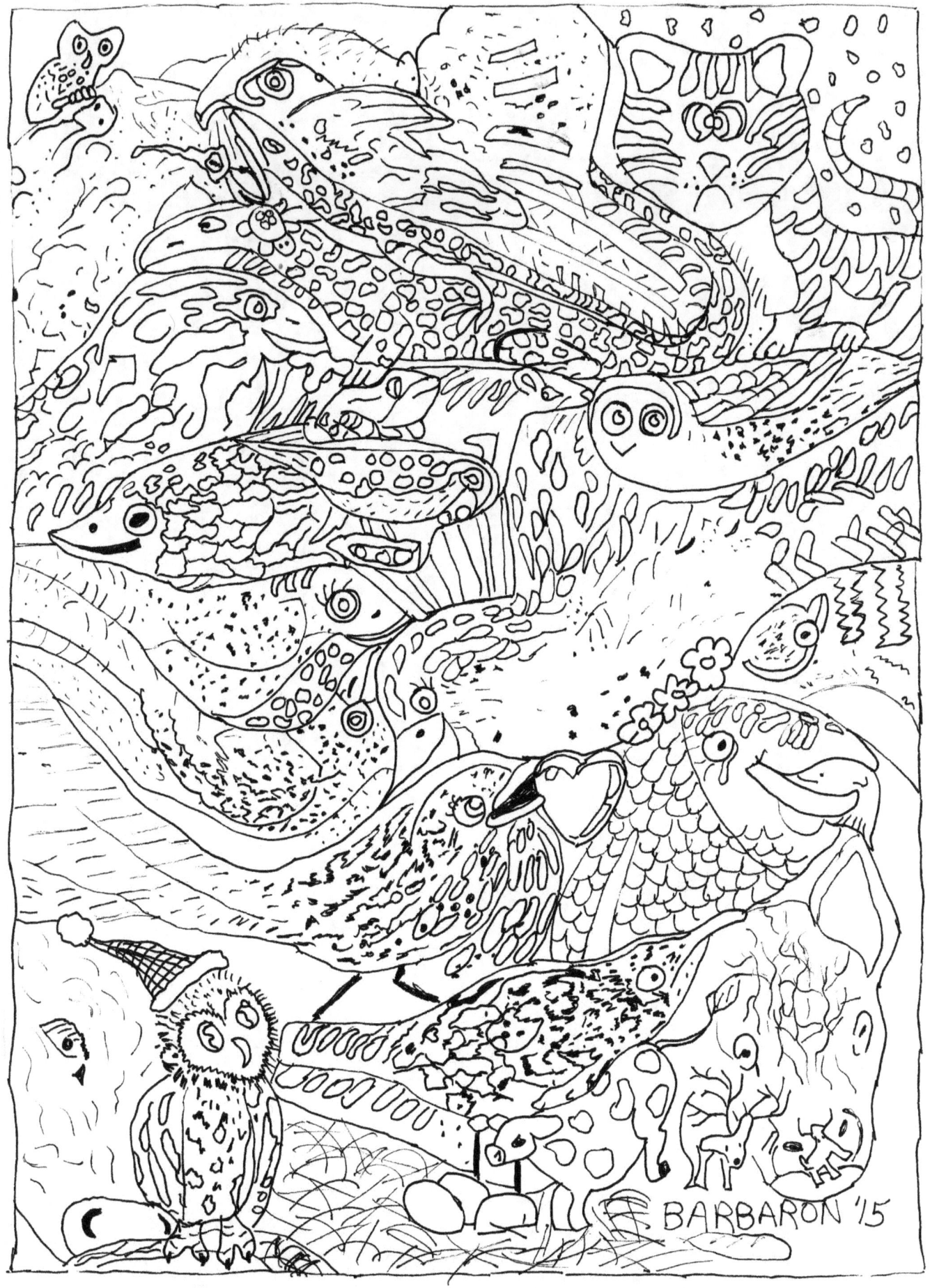

The Cross-Eyed Cat

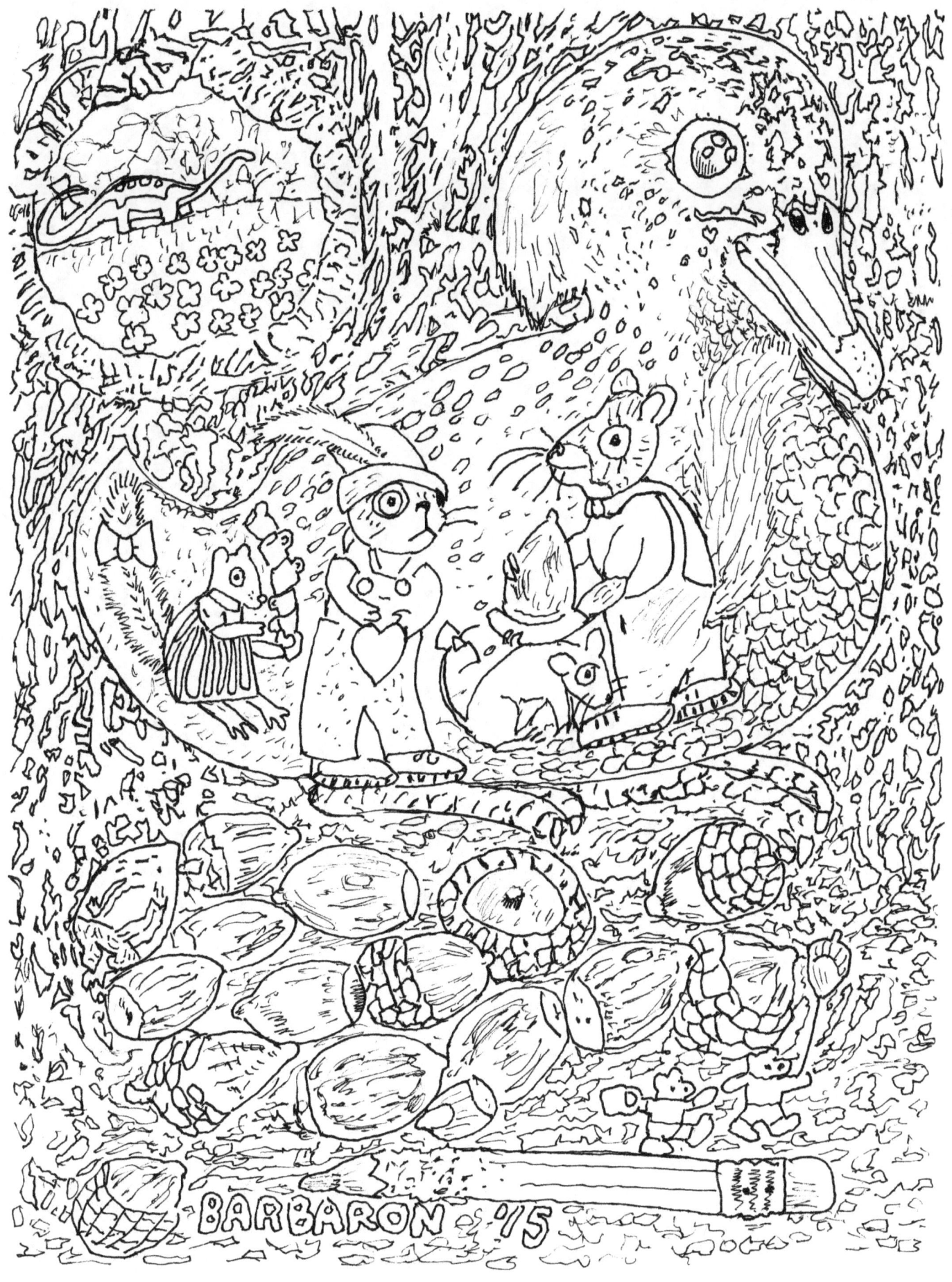

Mrs. Wood's Spring Cleaning

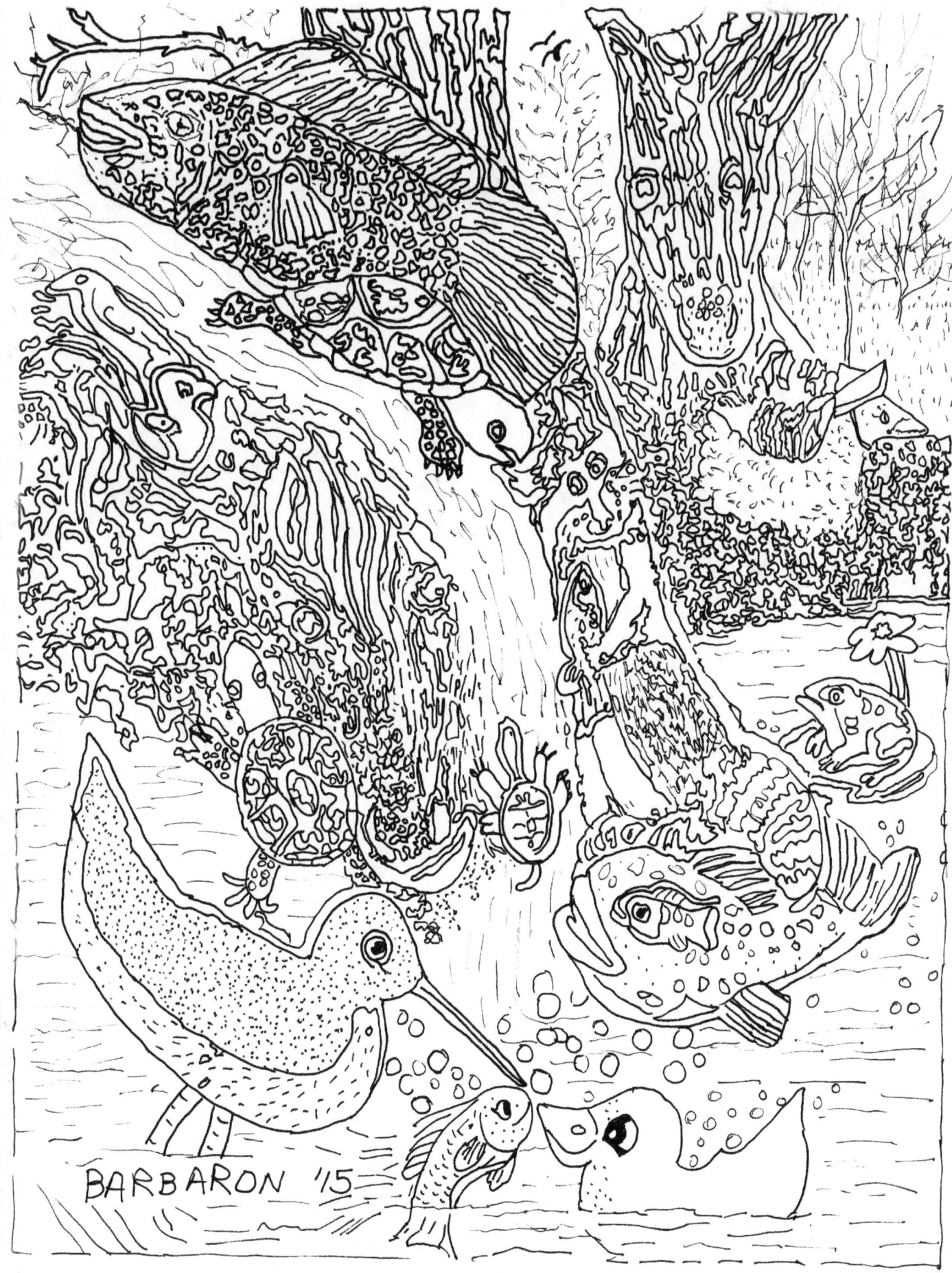

Cool Times at Turtle Falls

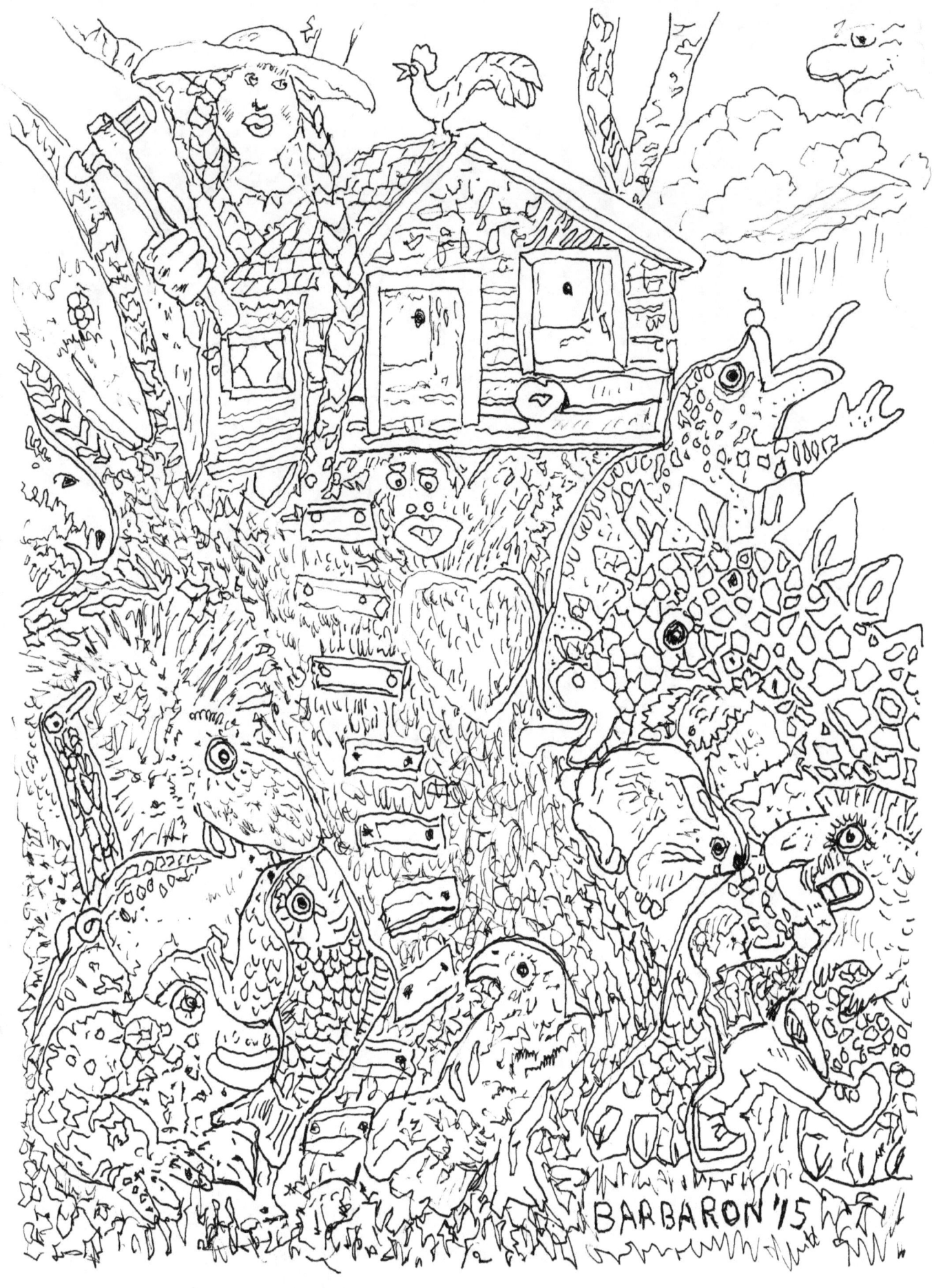

Mrs. Hammer Slammer's Tree House

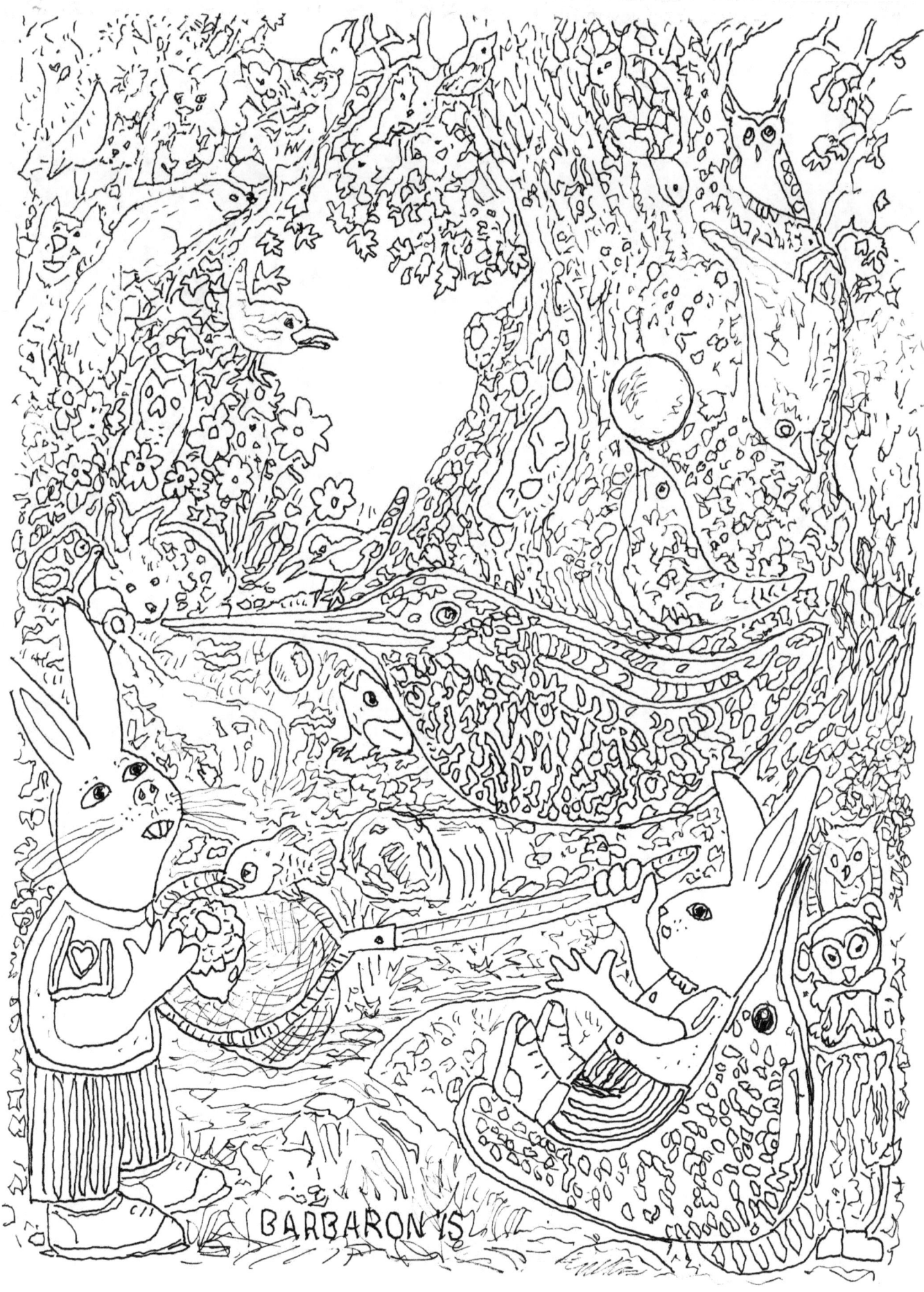

Mr. Green's Cool Shade Tree

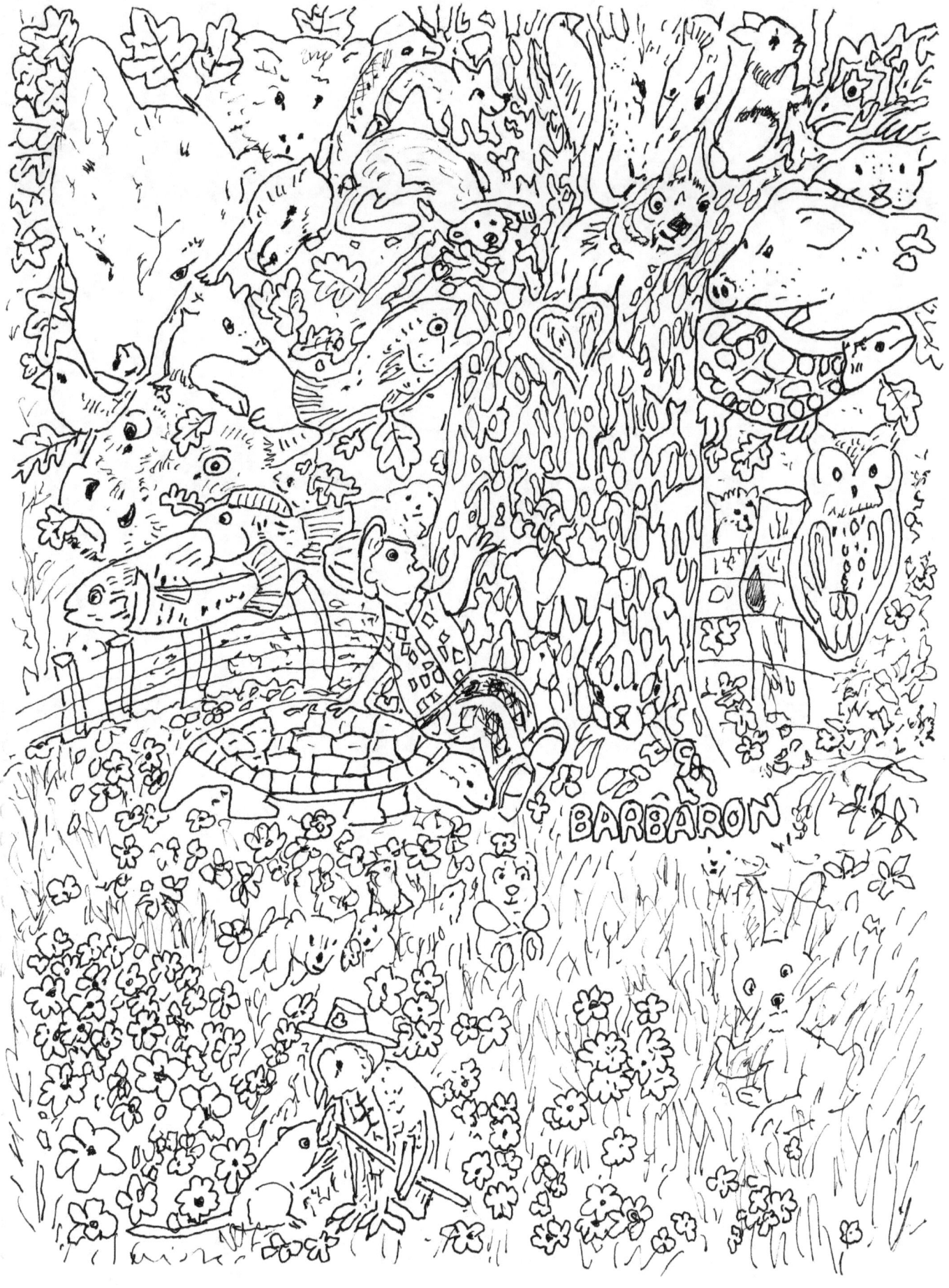

The Whispering Oak

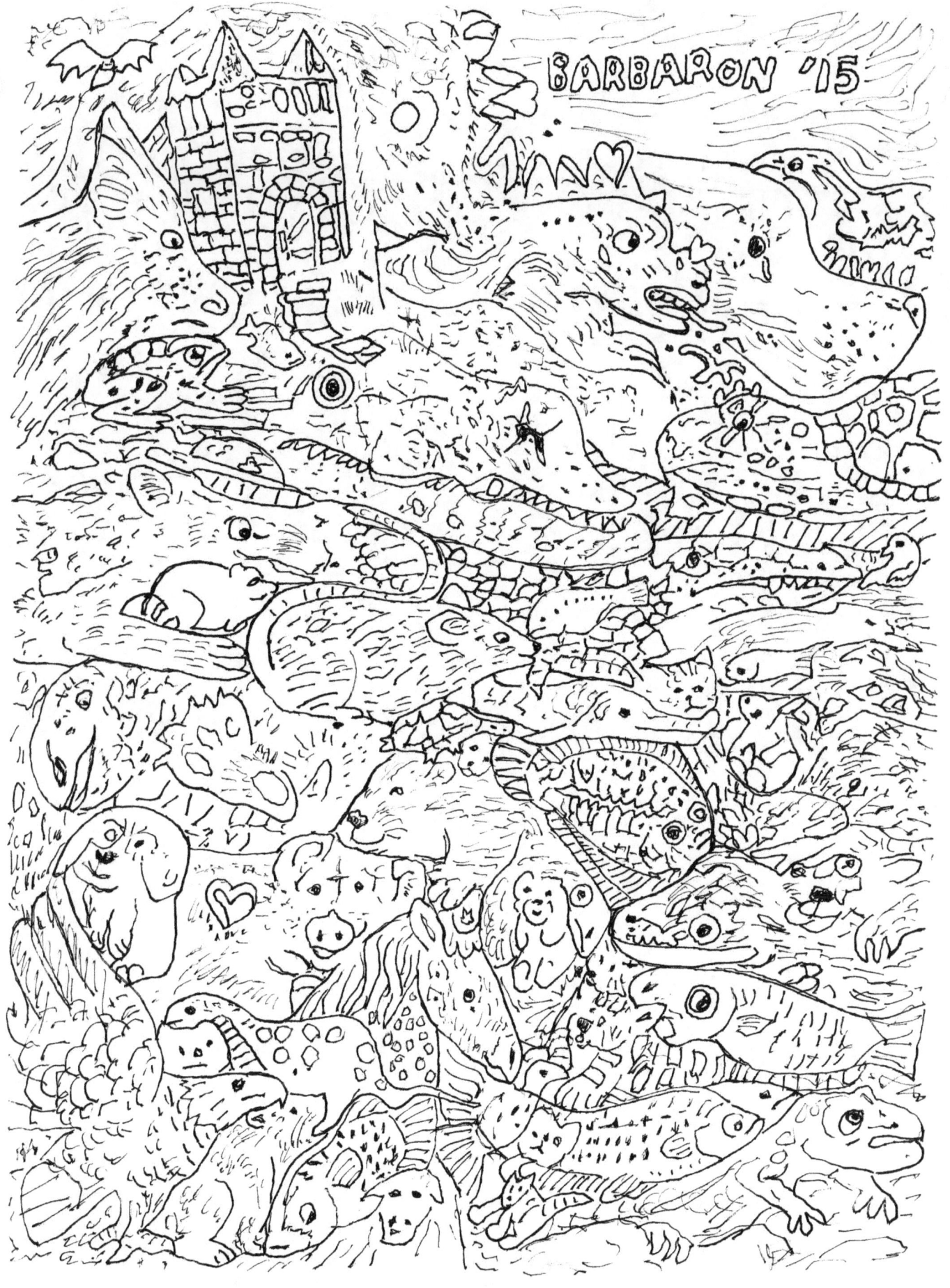

Stay Out of the King's Mote!

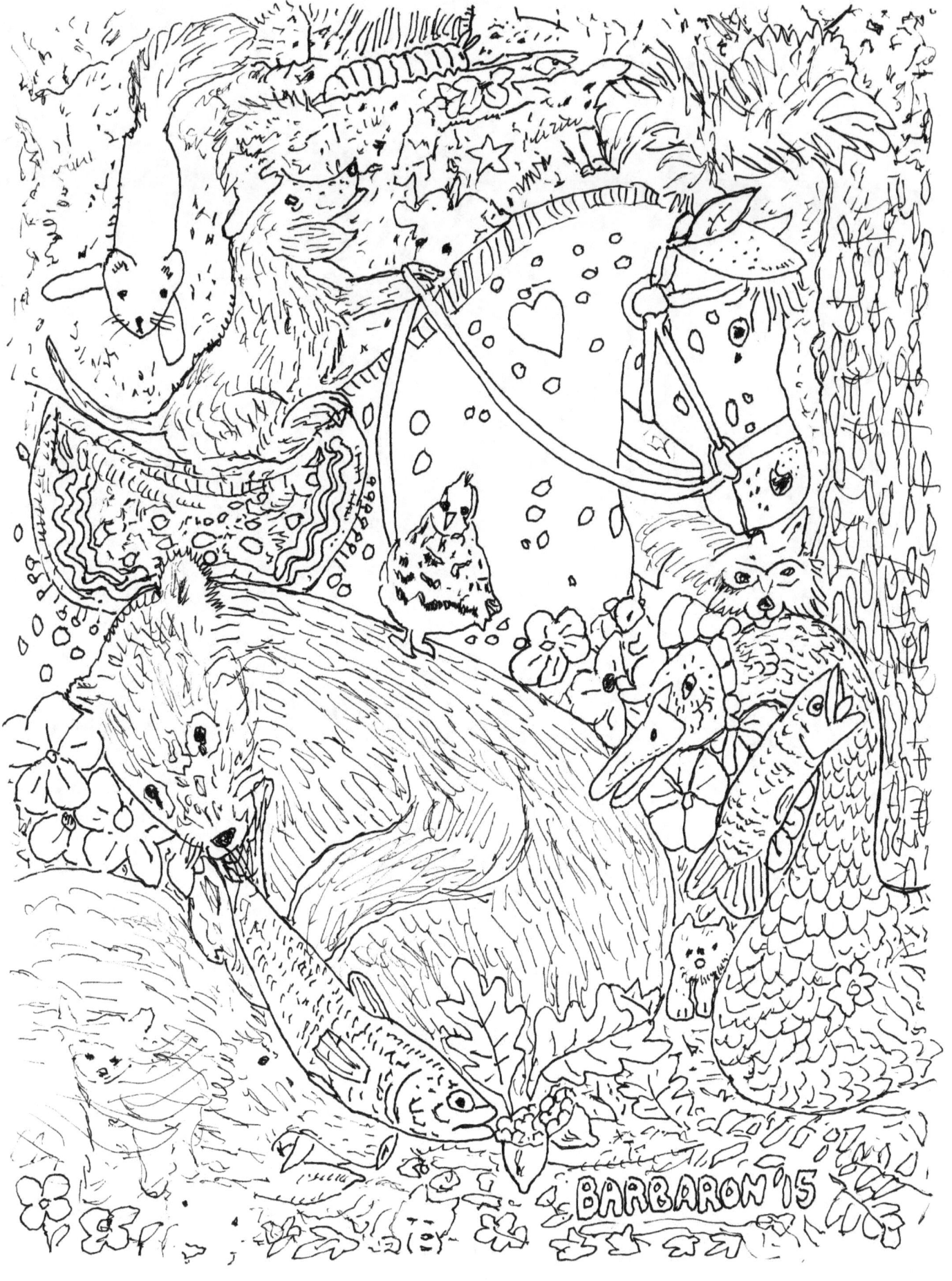

White House Parade

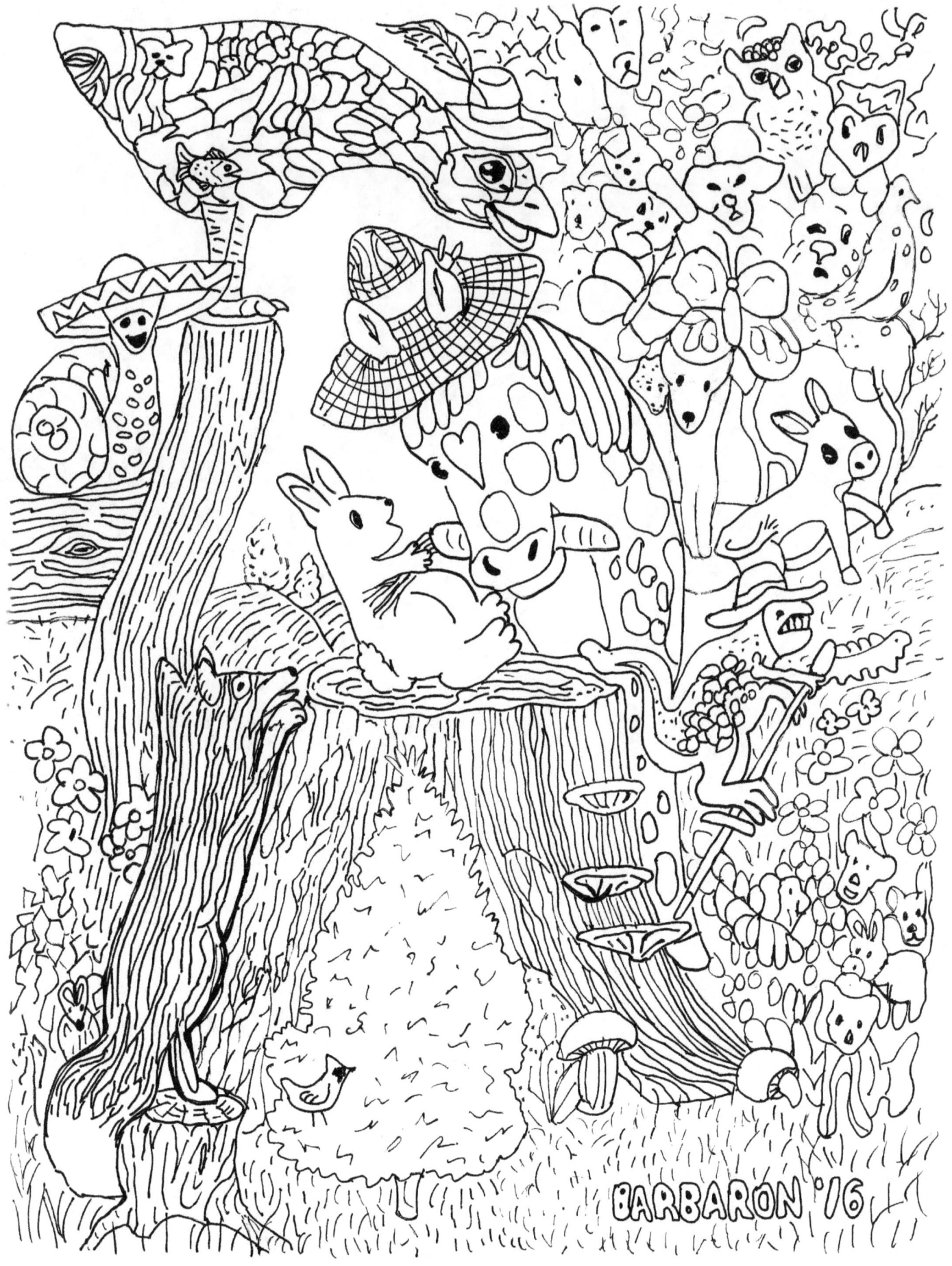

A Carrot for Miss-Green-with-White-Spots

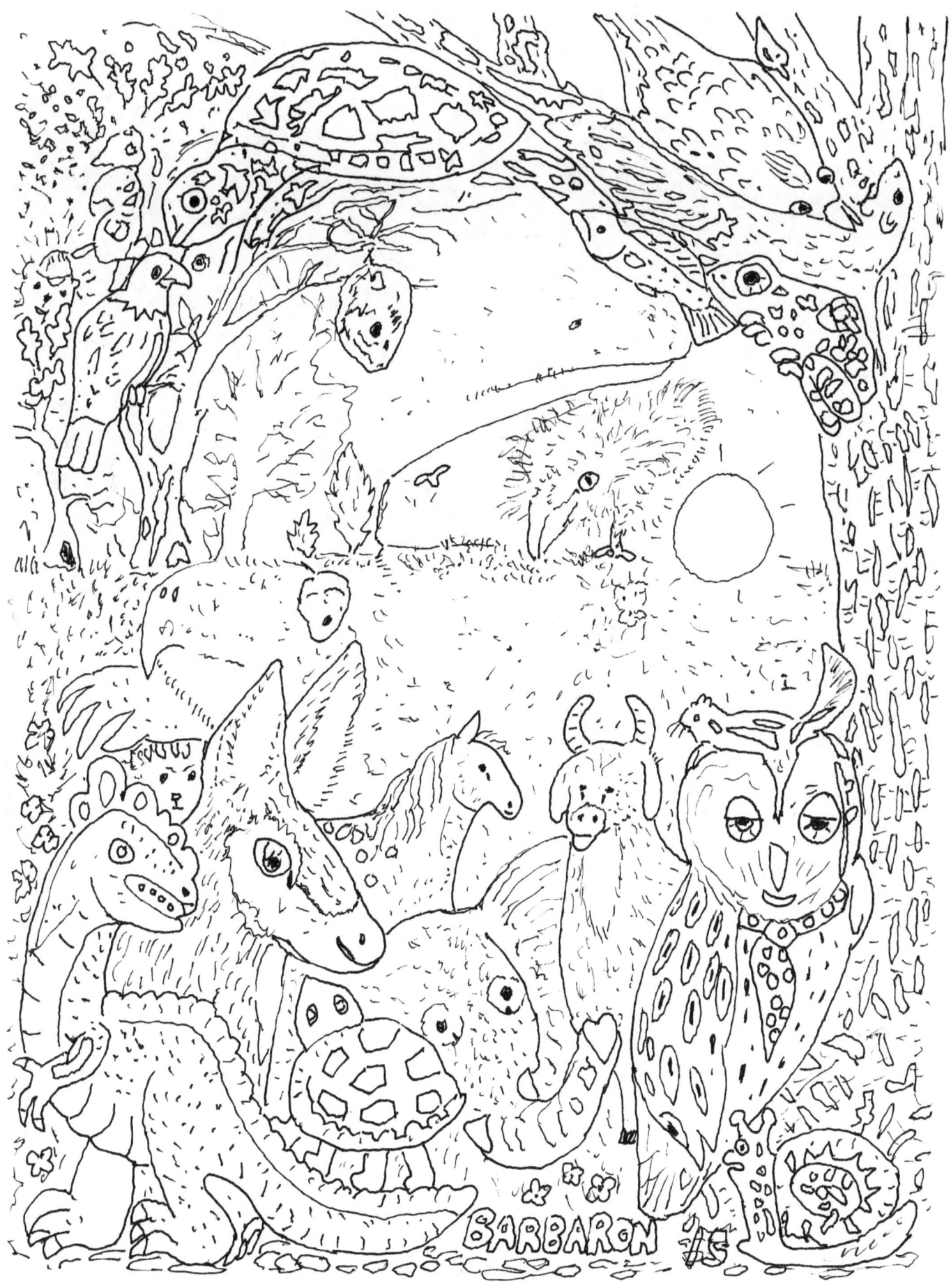

Snail's Big News

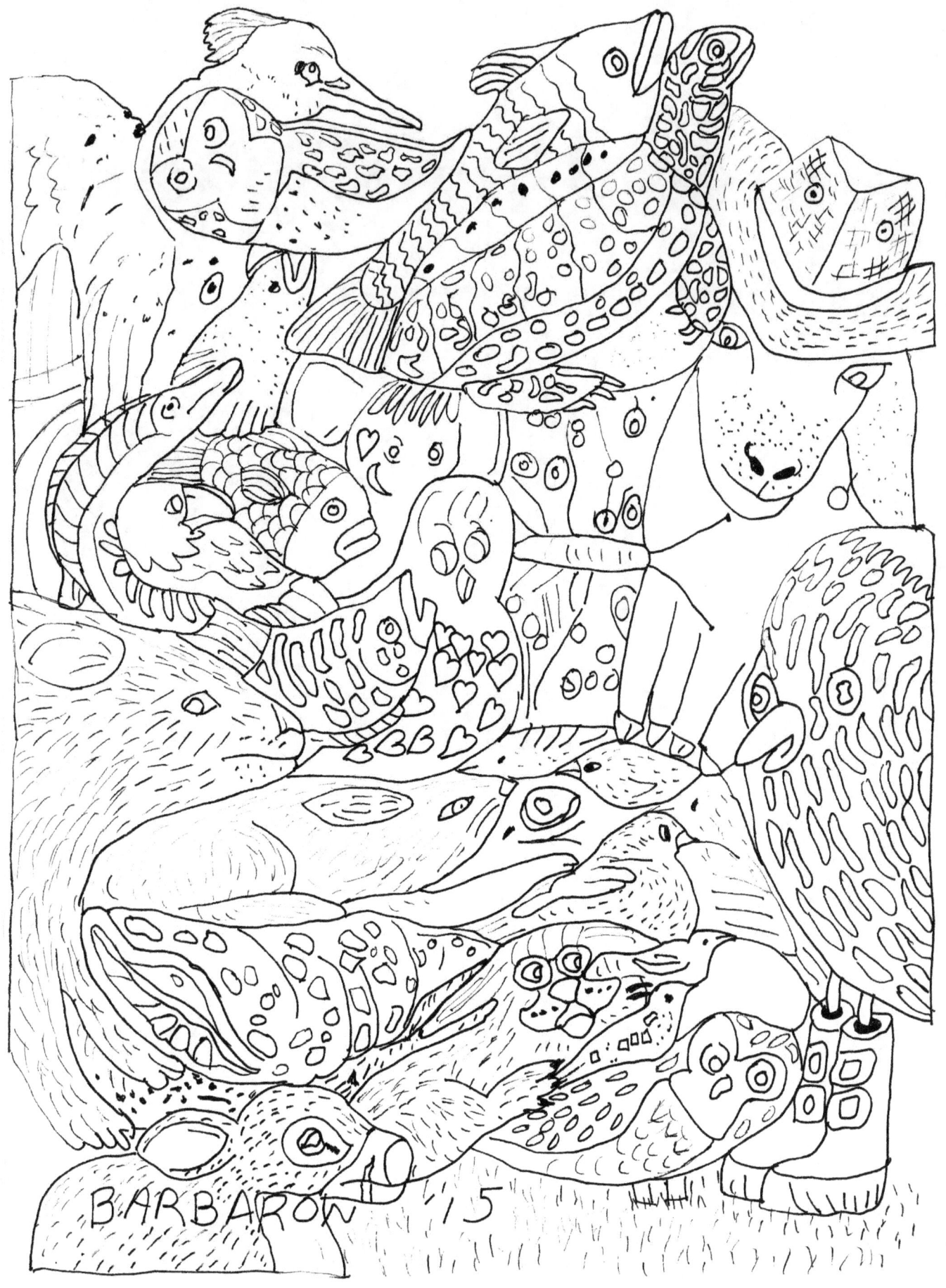

Kid with the Purple Hat

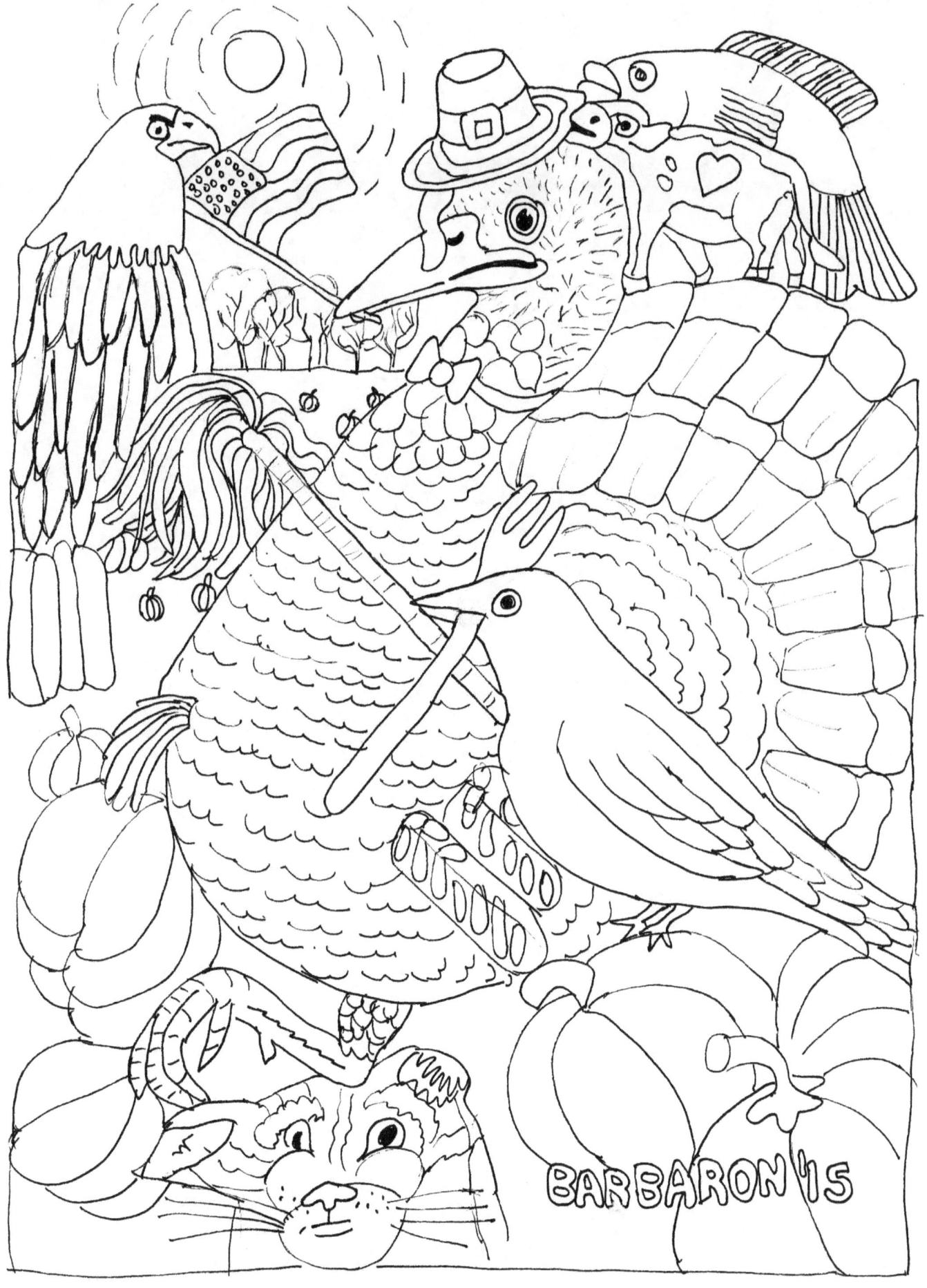

Pumpkin Patch Parade

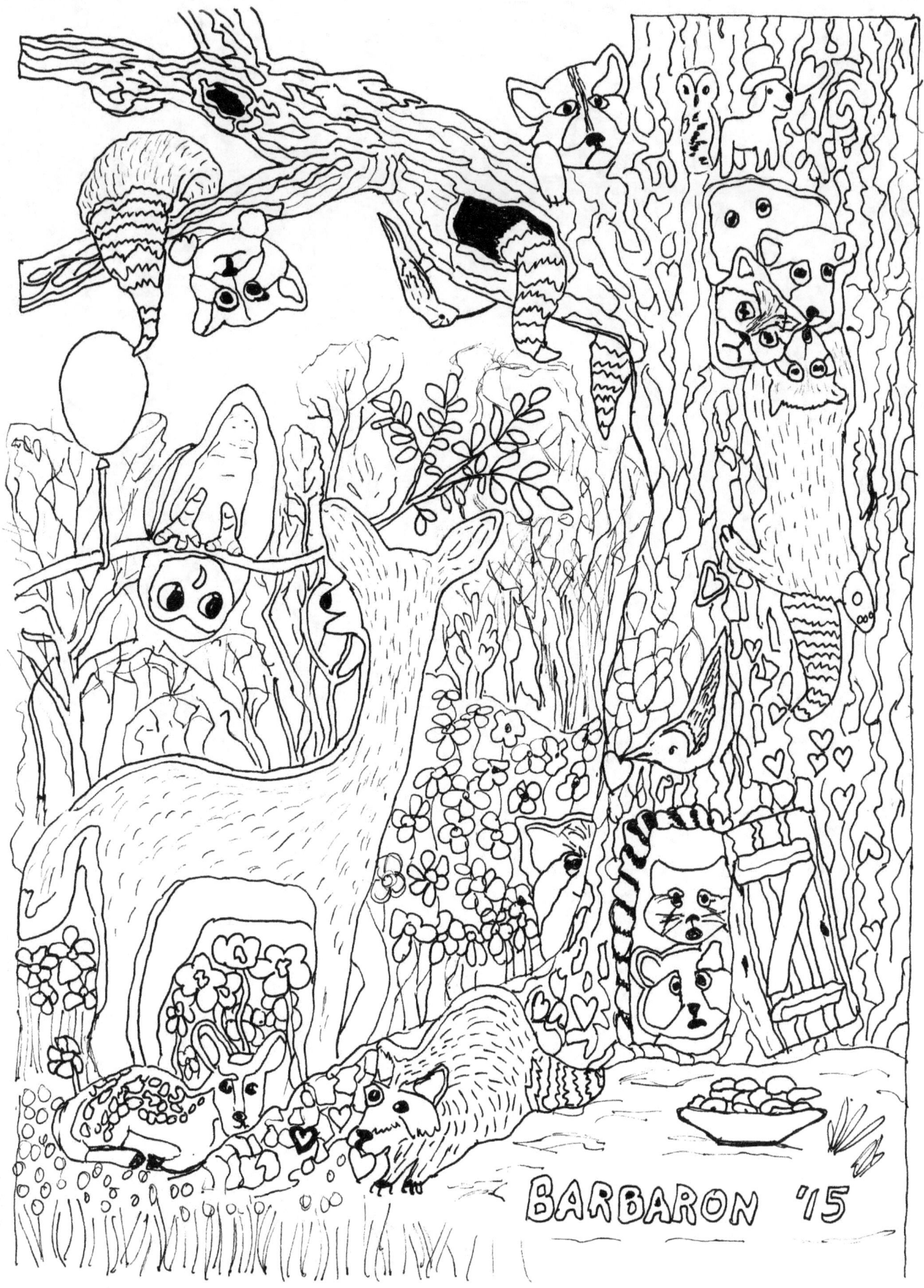

Birth Day Cookie Party

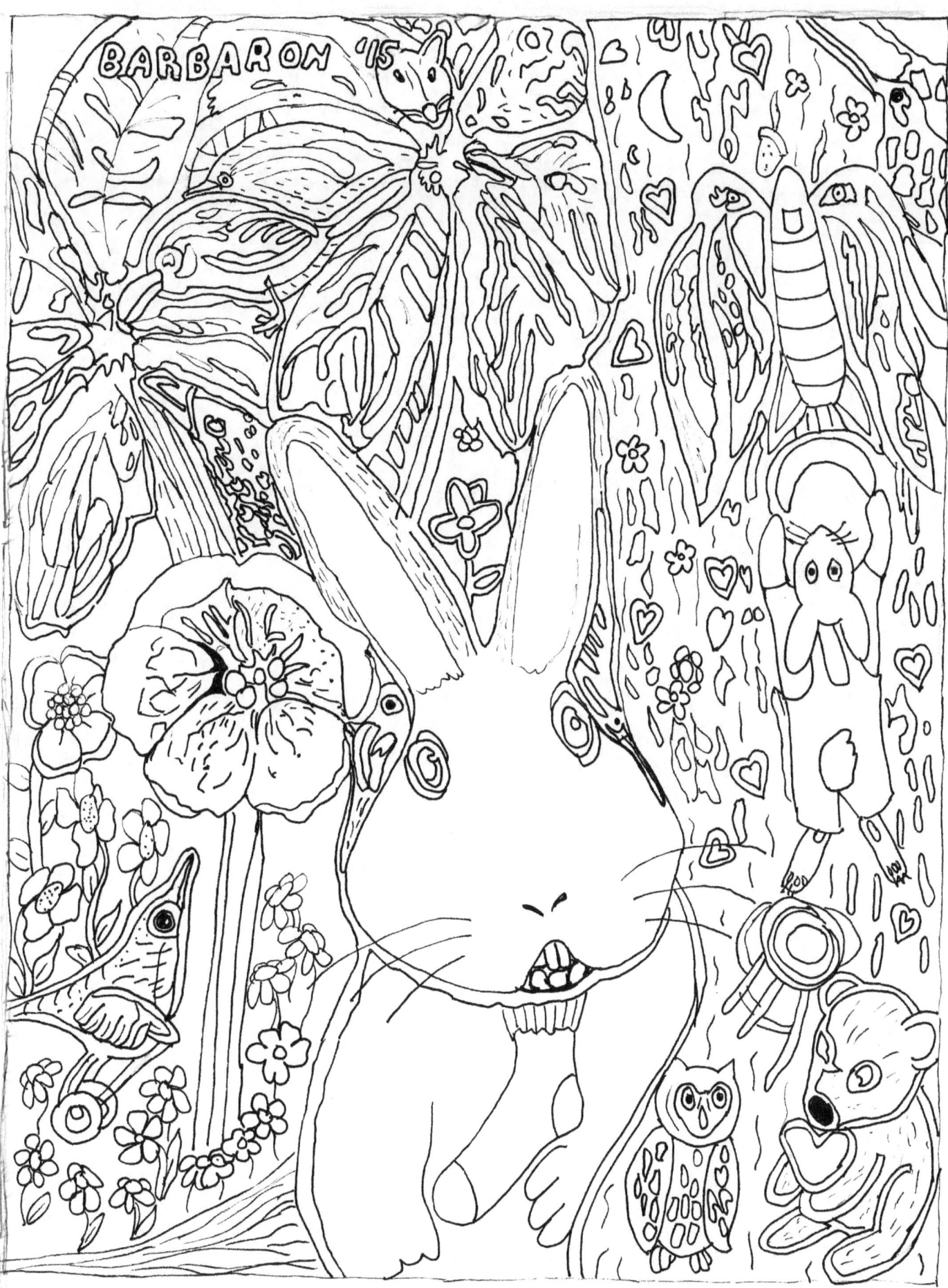

Blue Bunny's Ordinary Day

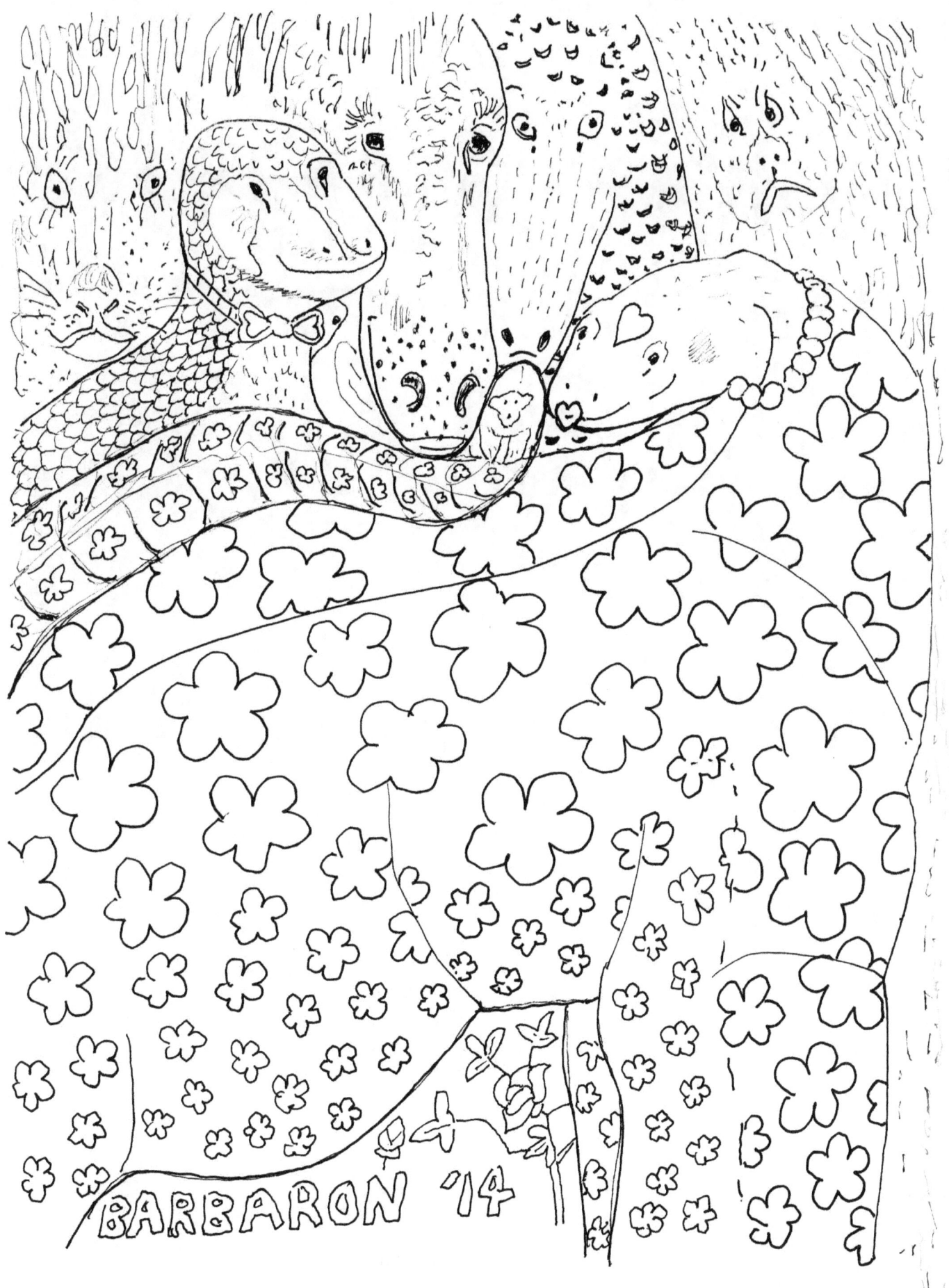

Pinkie with Pearls

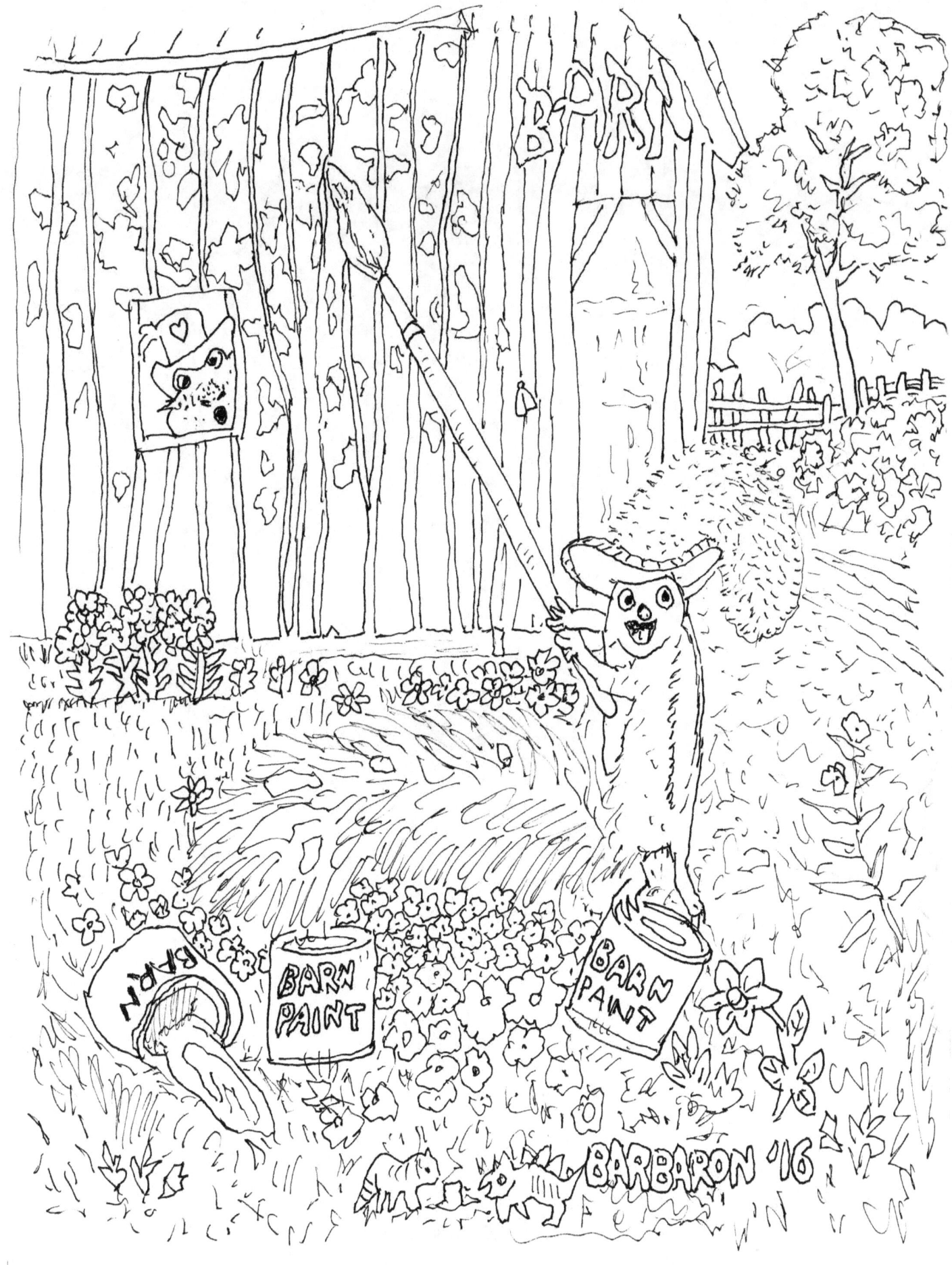

Skunk Paints the Barn